In Her Place

By Shirley Schroeder

First Edition

Biographical Publishing Company
Prospect, Connecticut

In Her Place
First Edition

Published by:

Biographical Publishing Company
95 Sycamore Drive
Prospect, CT 06712-1493

Phone: 203-758-3661   Fax: 253-793-2618
e-mail: biopub@aol.com

All rights reserved. No part of this book may be reproduced or transmitted in any form or by any means, electronic or mechanical, including photocopying, recording, or by any information storage or retrieval system without the written permission of the author, except for the inclusion of brief quotations in a review.

Copyright © 2011 by Shirley Schroeder
Second Printing 2012

PRINTED IN THE UNITED STATES OF AMERICA

Publisher's Cataloging-in-Publication Data

Schroeder, Shirley.
In Her Place/ by Shirley Schroeder.
1st ed.
p. cm.
ISBN 1-929882-63-7 (alk. Paper)
13-Digit ISBN 978-1-929882-63-2
1. Title. 2. Biography. 3. Germany. 4. United States.
5. Farm Life.
Dewey Decimal Classification: 920 Biography
Library of Congress Control Number: 2011907291

TABLE OF CONTENTS

Author's Note 5
Memories 6
Chapter One – Christmas Eve 9
Chapter Two – Good Bye 10
Chapter Three – Out to Sea 11
Chapter Four – America 12
Chapter Five – Wrong Destination 14
Chapter Six – The Becker Farm 16
Chapter Seven – Hard Work 18
Chapter Eight – Confirmation Class 21
Chapter Nine – Problems with Paul 24
Chapter Ten Early Morning Duty 25
Chapter Eleven – Few Bright Spots 26
Chapter Twelve – Move to the City 28
Chapter Thirteen – The Clark's 30
Chapter Fourteen – Dan 32
Chapter Fifteen – Our Own Place 35
Chapter Sixteen – A Farmer's Wife 38
Chapter Seventeen – Old Mr. Grump 41
Chapter Eighteen – Our Son, Harvey 42
Chapter Nineteen – Pa's Teasing 44
Chapter Twenty – Our Son, Leslie 45
Chapter Twenty One – Walking in a Storm 47
Chapter Twenty Two – Gretchen 48
Chapter Twenty Three – Money Trouble 51
Chapter Twenty Four – The Accusation 53
Chapter Twenty Five – Harvey Starts School 57
Chapter Twenty Six – Pa Dies 59
Chapter Twenty Seven – Gretchen Marries 61
Chapter Twenty Eight – Our Daughter, Shirley 62
Chapter Twenty Nine – Harvest Time 64
Chapter Thirty – Our Daughter, Carol 67
Chapter Thirty One – Citizenship 69
Chapter Thirty Two – Accused of Stealing 71
Chapter Thirty Three – Bad Habits 75

Chapter Thirty Four – Dan's Injury 77
Chapter Thirty Five – Family Reunion 79
Chapter Thirty Six – My Garden 81
Chapter Thirty Seven – Aunt Greta 83
Chapter Thirty Eight – Gretchen Divorces 85
Chapter Thirty Nine – Hired Hands 87
Chapter Forty – The Storm 89
Chapter Forty One – Hay Fever 92
Chapter Forty Two – Mother's Day 94
Chapter Forty Three – A Misunderstanding 97
Chapter Forty Four – Up North 101
Chapter Forty Five – Christmas Melancholy 105
Chapter Forty Six – Rusty 107
Chapter Forty Seven – Fire 110
Chapter Forty Eight – Leslie 113
Chapter Forty Nine – Harvey 115
Chapter Fifty – The Girls Move West 116
Chapter Fifty One – House on the Lake 119
Chapter Fifty Two – Double Wedding 121
Chapter Fifty Three – My First Grandchild 124
Chapter Fifty Four – Precious Moments 125
Chapter Fifty Five – Shirley's New Home 127
Chapter Fifty Six – Divorced 130
Chapter Fifty Seven – Dog Trouble 131
Chapter Fifty Eight – Changes on the Farm 133
Chapter Fifty Nine – Dan's Illness 137
Chapter Sixty – What I Have Left 140
Chapter Sixty One – Another Grandson 142
Chapter Sixty Two – First Signs 144
Chapter Sixty Three – Last Days 145
Chapter Sixty Four – To Sleep 148
Author's Epilog 149
A Final Word from the Author 150

AUTHOR'S NOTE

This book is based on the true story of my mother's life from my perspective. Of necessity, some parts have been added, changed or even fictionalized to make them more complete. Some names have been changed to protect the innocent.

MEMORIES

Through a misty haze I'm riding on Papa's shoulder. There are people – lots of people. And music. Violin music. My uncle is playing a lively jig on his violin. Papa boasts about how I've grown. How pretty I am.

~ ~ ~

Grandma holds me on her big, soft lap and hugs me close. I know she and Grandpa love me.

~ ~ ~

Mama opens the door. A man hands her a piece of paper. She stares at it, her hand goes up to her mouth, her shoulders shake and she steps to the couch to sit down. Papa is dead. He was a soldier in the war but did not die in battle. He died in a hospital of complications from pneumonia.

~ ~ ~

It's hard for me, my two brothers and sister now that Papa's gone. Mama is meaner than ever. Often when I get home from school, she hits me on the head with a stick. Says I'm late getting home, but I'm not. I cringe, cover my head with my arms, run to my room and shut the door. Fredrick, Gretchen and Hans escape the stick. She takes her anger out on me – the oldest.

~ ~ ~

I grab Fredrick by the hair and scold him for letting the chickens out again. He forgets to close the gate after himself and I'm tired of reminding him. He squeals as I shake his head and promises to remember the gate from now on.

~ ~ ~

I have to stay with Aunt Belle for a while. Mama is sick and in a sanitarium. She coughs a lot and is very weak. Fredrick, Gretchen and Hans are all at different homes until Mama is better.

~ ~ ~

I wake up. It's dark. I hear muffled sounds from Mama's bedroom. A low man's voice is talking. Mama answers and laughs. I listen and wonder. Can't sleep while the man is in our house. Soon I hear his footsteps in the hall. The back door opens and shuts. I rise from my goose down bed and peer out the window. The man slinks along the side of the house, looks both ways and walks swiftly away. He's gone. Now I can sleep.

~ ~ ~

It's late. I can't sleep. Aunt Belle and Mama are talking. Mama says, "I can't make ends meet this way. Greta has offered to take the girls. That would leave me with just the boys and I could probably make it."

Aunt Belle says, "I thought Herman was close to proposing to you." "No," Mama says. "He didn't exactly say it, but a widow is one thing. A widow with four children quite another."

Mama, baby Hans, Me, Fredrick and Gretchen (in the buggy)

CHAPTER ONE

"Christmas Eve"

It's Christmas Eve, 1922. Huge snowflakes drift lazily to the ground as I walk through my little village of Wurchow, Germany, to the church on the hill. I look up at the dark sky, then close my eyes and let the snowflakes fall on my face. I stick out my tongue to taste their coolness. Skipping along the snow-packed road, I stare ahead at the bright lights of the church. How lovely the steeple looks with the snowflakes falling around it. Coming here makes me feel at peace and I like to hear about the love of God.

Things have been hard since Papa died five years ago. When he had been around, Mama was kinder. I try to forget the sadness over Papa being gone. After all, it's Christmas Eve. I should be happy. Maybe Mama will like the shawl I've knit for her gift. She's so hard to please. Always was but it is worse since Papa died.

When I reach the church steps, I hear the children's choir already rehearsing. I'm late again. Emma won't like it. We're both in seventh grade at school and best friends. If only Fredrick could have cleared the table and washed the dishes once. But, no, I had to finish while everyone else got ready even though I was the only one who had to leave early. I take my place next to Emma. The frown on her face turns into a smile when I stick my tongue out at her and join in the last line of "O Little Town of Bethlehem."

Emma and I whisper and giggle through most of that Christmas Eve service, neither one knowing it'd be the last we'd ever spend together.

CHAPTER TWO

"Good Bye"

July 23, 1923, Gretchen and I stand on the dock huddling close together and stare at Mama, Fredrick and Hans. We say goodbye and everyone hugs each other. Gretchen begins to cry, "I don't want to go to America, Mama. I want to stay here with you."

"There, there," Mama says, "Heidi will take good care of you and Aunt Greta and Uncle Alfred have lots of boys and girls for you to play with. You will like it in rich America. Everyone there has fine clothes and cream and honey on the table. Now, hush. No more tears."

I hang back from Mama and watch the people going up the ramp. I touch the nametag on my lapel and hope I won't lose the money bills Mama gave me. I know what to do. Watch Gretchen the two weeks on the boat. When we arrive in America I have to keep a close eye on her until Aunt Greta comes to get us. Oh, how I will miss Emma. But Emma promised to write. We will always, always be friends – no matter how far we are apart.

A loud blast from the ship's horn makes me jump. Everyone around us shuffles towards the ramp and Gretchen and I are swept along with them. I take Gretchen's hand and try to look back at my family. Will I ever see them again?

CHAPTER THREE

"Out to Sea"

The trip on the S.S. Finland from Hamburg, Germany to Boston, Massachusetts, America, takes two weeks. When the boat rolls and tosses in the huge waves, I lie in my bunk too ill to raise my head. On the calmer days, I am able to leave the small room and explore the boat.

When I walk about the boat, it seems like a huge building with many interesting rooms. On the top deck there are things to do so Gretchen and I play ball. Once I reached over the railing to get the ball and looked down at the water whooshing by. I leaped away from the railing, afraid of how fast the boat moved and of how deep the waters must be.

The rolling and tossing does not affect Gretchen so she runs around the boat every day. When I can't watch her, I pray God will take care of her. And then I pray for calmer waters and the journey to end.

Occasionally I try to eat but usually just the thought of food makes me feel worse so I eat very little.

As the boat eases into the protected waters of Boston, my seasickness eases and I thank God for a safe journey.

CHAPTER FOUR

"America"

Back on land, I don't feel ill anymore. I look at my surroundings while Gretchen and I stand in line. We enter a large, low building with crowds of people ahead and behind. The girl nearest turns and smiles at me. She has long brown hair and large friendly brown eyes. She is tall and dressed in a flowered linen dress. She says in German, "Hello. My name is Anne. Did you enjoy the boat ride?"

Wow! Someone speaking in my language. How wonderful to understand what she is saying. I shake my head and say, "I was ill a lot of the time and only saw the four walls of our small room. I'm happy to be back on solid ground."

We move through the line. Anne and I continue to visit and soon discover we are to be on the same train destined for Wisconsin.

When we finish with the immigration officials, we board the train together. Gretchen and I sit on one side, Anne across from us. People are talking in what must be English. I don't understand a word they say. How refreshing to have Anne to talk to.

Anne asks, "Are you hungry?"

I nod and Anne hands me a strange yellow fruit. I've never seen such a thing before so I just stare at it. When I don't do anything, Anne asks, "Have you never seen a banana before?" I shake my head and Anne takes the banana by the end and begins to peel it. She offers the fruit to me and I hesitate a moment but take it. It has a strange taste something like a mushy apple. It does help take away my hunger. I give some to Gretchen.

While waiting for the train to leave the station, I look out the window and see the strangest man I've ever seen. He is black – all over – not from dirt either. He has a black face, black hands stick out from his tattered jacket. He is running. A white man is chasing him with an umbrella. The black man reaches a fence, jumps up on it and scrambles over just as the white man's umbrella comes down on the fence. I wonder what the poor black man did to deserve such treatment.

As the train slowly leaves the station, I stare out the window at my new homeland. I try not to blink so I won't miss anything. When the train speeds up, the buildings whiz by. It seems we are in the city for a long, long time and when we leave it, I see rich green farmland, much like the land in Germany only more of it, much more.

CHAPTER FIVE

"Wrong Destination"

We are supposed to get off in Neenah, Wisconsin, but we don't. I can't leave Anne, the only person who has been kind to us since arriving in America. I have to stay with her so Anne says, "OK, you come with me. We'll let your relatives know where you are when we reach Milwaukee."

When we reach the station in Milwaukee, Anne talks to the station attendant who sends a wire to Aunt Greta and Uncle Alfred explaining the situation and we leave with Anne.

Two days later, I look out the window in anticipation of our Aunt and Uncle to arrive. A horse and buggy pull into the driveway and two people get out. The man is tall and thin with a bushy mustache. He wears a tattered brown hat and helps a short, stocky lady with a pinched face down from the buggy. The woman is wearing a long black dress and her hair is pulled tightly back. She frowns as she looks around. My heart sinks as I watch these harsh-looking people walk up the sidewalk. There is a knock and Anne goes to answer the door.

"Are the Tesch girls from Germany here?" asks Uncle Alfred.

"Yes," answers Anne. "Come in."

Anne brings them into the living room where Gretchen and I are waiting.

"Well," Aunt Greta says when she sees us. "It's been a time findin' you two. Too bad we had to waste all this time when we should have been workin' at the farm. This yers?" she asks pointing to our trunk. I nod.

"Alfred, get it in the buggy," says Aunt Greta.

While Alfred loads our trunk, I hug Anne and say, "Goodbye. Thank you for your kindness."

"I'm glad I could help you, Heidi. May God go with you to your new home."

Gretchen and I sit close together in the buggy. We look at each other. I hug her and smooth her long blonde hair away from her face. When I see tears forming in her green eyes, I whisper, "It's OK. We'll be fine."

But I don't believe a word I'm saying. Not for a minute. Not with these harsh people. And yet in my heart I know we'll be OK. Somehow God will see that we are. He just has to.

CHAPTER SIX

"The Becker Farm"

The train ride from Milwaukee takes several hours. It is mid afternoon when we reach Neenah. A young man named Max meets us with a horse and buggy. He is short and stocky, much like Aunt Greta. I figure this must be their son. He has wavy blond hair, deep blue eyes and the first friendly smile I've seen from this family.

Aunt Greta says, "This here's Max. He's married now and works for the Jenkins on their farm."

We get in the buggy while Uncle Alfred and Max load our trunk.

It is late afternoon when we turn down a long lane. Max swings his arm out and says, "This here's all Becker land. Both sides. Thirty-five acres of good farmland. Pretty nice, huh?"

We drive up to a weather-beaten, once-white house. A gray barn stands off to one side with two smaller sheds behind. Tall grass surrounds the barn and sheds but the lawn around the house is well mowed. A small herd of black-and-white cows graze contentedly behind the buildings.

"I see Paul finally did get that lawn mowed, " says Aunt Greta. "Better have or he'd wish he had."

Aunt Greta no more says these words when a group of children burst out the door of the house and down the steps. They run towards us, all jabbering at once – some in German – some in English.

"Alright, alright, calm down," yells Aunt Greta. "No need to scare the girls."

One by one the six children introduce themselves, four boys, two girls. The boys are loud, the girls shy. I don't catch any of their names, only remember Max. I'm too busy staring at the tattered, barefoot human beings standing before me. This large family – all these people living on this sorry-looking old farm.

CHAPTER SEVEN

"Hard Work"

That night I toss and turn on a straw mattress in the small bedroom. Gretchen sleeps beside me even though the bed moves back and forth each time I turn. I try to stop the tears falling and pray for help from God to handle what's happened to us.

"Why, oh why did we have to come to such a place? Rich America," I whisper. "If this is rich, what must poor be?" Emma. How I miss her. Mama, Fredrick and Hans. How I miss them. But Emma. She's really the one I miss.

The next thing I know, bright sunshine is streaming through the dusty lace curtains on the window. I hear noises from the kitchen and poke Gretchen.

"We better get up and downstairs. Let's go."

When we walk in the kitchen, we see everyone sitting around the table.

"Sit here and here," says Aunt Greta. "And eat yer oatmeal."

No one talks at the table. They all eat and stare at me and Gretchen. All I can handle is two bites of the watery dish of oatmeal.

After everyone leaves, Aunt Greta tells me and Gretchen about our chores. Mostly we will follow Bernice and Margaret around and help them until we know what to do ourselves. Chickens and pigs have to be fed. Goats milked and fed. When these animals are taken care of, we return to the house to clear the table and wash the dishes. When the dishes are finished, we are to help wash the clothes. We learn how many pails of water to haul in and how to use the scrub board.

While working, I tell Margaret about my life in Germany – how different it was. Margaret is three years older and seems nicer than anyone else.

When the house chores are finished, we turn to the garden to pull weeds. It takes some learning to know the difference between the weeds and the plants and Gretchen and I are scolded several times for pulling out the wrong thing.

Lunch time we again receive watery oatmeal and bread with lard spread on it.

After lunch we go back outside to finish pulling weeds. Later, before supper, we again take care of the animals.

Supper is fried potatoes with onion and small bits of meat. That first night we each got an apple.

This scene is repeated every day but Sunday. No work is done that day except to feed the animals and milk the cows and goats. We all dress in our best clothes, pile into two buggies, one driven by Uncle Alfred, the other by Max and go to Trinity Lutheran Church in Neenah – four miles from the farm.

On Sunday the house is full of extra people because all the married children come home for dinner. There's hardly any room around the table but somehow we all squeeze in. There are four more couples, two young men and too many little ones to count. Sunday dinner is the best meal all week – chicken with potatoes and gravy, a vegetable of peas or green beans and a dessert of cookies or cake. But we only get a small portion. I'm always hungry, always. At no time can I eat as much as I want.

Margaret and I often talk before bedtime. Margaret is a good listener and tries to encourage me. She tells me she knows her Mama seems like a harsh person but underneath it all, she really has a warm heart. I nod but don't believe a word she tells me. I need to see some kind of proof before I'll believe her.

As the weeks go by, I also learn how to help in the barn. I feed the cows and shovel manure. I gather hay in the field and harvest vegetables from the garden. But few vegetables are eaten by the family. Most are sold at the farmer's market each week.

At night when I don't talk with Margaret, I write to Emma. I tell her how much I miss her and Germany. And how I wonder why, oh why, Gretchen and I are in America in the first place. Things were so much better in Germany than they are here. There was always enough food to eat. And variety. Not the same old thing every day. I slept on a goose down mattress, not straw like here.

Now and then I write to Mama, Fredrick and Hans but mainly I write to Emma. I never tell Mama how bad I feel, only Emma. I give the letters to Aunt Greta to mail. The first time I get a letter from Emma, it is already open when I get it. Questioning Aunt Greta, she says, "I need to know what you're writin' to these people back in Germany. Better be nothin' but good comin' from you when you think about the good care you're gettin' from us."

I stare at her and wonder if Aunt Greta opened my letters she mailed for me too. If she had, she would have learned that I had nothing good to say about my life in America. But the way Aunt Greta talks, she must not have read the ones I already sent or I'd have been punished long ago. And yet, Aunt Greta's beady eyes bore through me when she tells me why she'd opened Emma's letter. Now I will have to be more careful what I write. My heart sinks because writing about my hard life to Emma seemed to somehow ease the pain.

CHAPTER EIGHT

"Confirmation Class"

One night after supper, Aunt Greta calls me into the living room. She motions to me to sit and says, "School will be starting soon. You will go with yer cousins. But you need to go to Confirmation Class every Wednesday too. Now, you know where the church is cuz we go nearly every Sunday but only the first time will Alfred take you. After that you walk. It's not all that far once you know the way."

I nod and get up from the couch. This was the first talk I've had alone with Aunt Greta and I see there isn't any talking back and forth. I just get to listen.

That night I talk with Margaret about Confirmation Class and school. She tells me she was confirmed three years ago and remembers the class means learning many Bible and hymn verses. "You'll like Pastor Schafer. He speaks English but translates into German. He is a good teacher and fun," she says.

"About school," Margaret goes on. "You stay close to Albert and Fred. They'll help you. Best thing for you to do is learn English as fast as you can. Hey, let's you and I talk English at home here instead of German. That will help. What do you think?"

"Well," I stammer, "I suppose we could try it."

Gretchen and I find school intolerable because of the language difference. The children poke fun at us, tease us, mimic German and I soon learn it's best to stay as quiet as possible. I don't understand a thing the teacher says but I do understand the arithmetic problems written on the board. Albert sits next to me and Fred sits next to Gretchen and say the English in German so we understand.

During school hours things aren't so bad but at recess time, the mocking and teasing is merciless. The boys especially poke fun at me I guess because I'm older. They babble in what they consider German to be.

It does no good to cry about any of this. I just must learn the English words. At recess Albert is off with the other boys speaking English. I feel so alone.

When Uncle Alfred takes me to my first Confirmation Class, I make sure to watch every turn so I'll remember how to get back to the farm.

Pastor Schafer is a kind man who speaks both English and German. He explains things when I don't understand the English words and I like him. This looks like something to look forward to – Confirmation Class on Wednesdays.

The first time I walk home everything is fine. But the second time, as I pass the Jenkin's farm, their big, black, hairy dog runs after me, growling and barking. No one comes to get him so I try to talk to him. It does no good so I back away, turn and run. The dog follows and bites me on the leg and then turns and runs back to the farm. I walk home as fast as I can. When I get there, I quickly go to the sink to wash up. But Aunt Greta sees the blood and asks, "What happened?" I tell her about the dog and she says, "You musta provoked him or somethin'. He's never done that before. Next time leave him alone and he'll leave you alone."

That night I wake up and feel like I've wet the bed. I quickly go into the small room where a porcelain pot sits for use at night. During the day we all use the outhouse down a small lane behind the house. When I check my pajamas I see blood.

"Oh, no, now what? Did that dog bite me more than on my leg? I fell when he attacked me but I didn't think he bit me more than once. Maybe if I wipe again it will be OK. Oh, no. I'm still bleeding." I start to cry.

"Heidi," whispers Margaret. "Is that you? What's the matter?"

"Oh, something's really wrong. I'm bleeding to death."

Margaret opens the door to the small room and comes in. She looks at my problem and smiles.

"Oh, Heidi, you're not dying. That's just your sick time. Don't you know about that?"

"Sick time? What are you talking about?"

"Guess nobody told you, huh? Well, every month about the same time you'll bleed like this but it quits in four to five days until the next month. You're fine. Here, I'll get you some of my rags to wear to catch the blood. You'll have to make some of your own tomorrow."

I stop crying and wonder what else bad is going to happen to me.

The next Wednesday when I come near the Jenkin's farm I walk slowly, a piece of bread held tightly in my hand. I have to make friends with this animal or forever be afraid to walk past this farm. When the dog comes running at me, I stand still and talk softly, extending my hand with the bread. When the dog sees the bread, he stops in his tracks, trots up to me and sniffs it. Then he takes it from my hand and while he eats, I slowly walk away. The dog does not follow. The next Wednesday, I do the same and we soon become friends.

CHAPTER NINE

"Problems with Paul"

One day on my way to feed the chickens, Paul catches up to me and puts his arm around my waist. I back away but Paul pulls me to him and whispers, "Hey, Heidi, come on in the barn with me. If you let me do what I want, I'll give you this candy bar." I shove him away and say, "No. Now leave me alone or I'll tell Uncle Alfred."

Paul moves closer and says with a wry grin, "Aw, come on, it'll be fun for both of us. You know, boy-girl kind of fun. Nobody will see us in the barn."

I turn and walk away blushing from ear to ear. No way am I doing any boy-girl stuff with Paul or any other boy.

After my next Confirmation Class I tell Pastor Schafer about Paul and what he said. Pastor tells me to stay clear of him or any other boy who talks this way. If Paul tries anything again, I'm to tell Uncle Alfred as I warned Paul I'd do.

A week later, as I come from feeding the chickens, I see Gretchen walking along eating a candy bar.

CHAPTER TEN

"Early Morning Duty"

Late that fall the weather got colder. One night after supper, Aunt Greta grabs me by my arm and says, "From now on, you'll be the one to get up in the morning and get the fire going. Then you can start breakfast. I'll call when you're to get up. See that you come soon as you're called."

Each morning from then on, I awake to Aunt Greta's, "Heidi! Get up!" It isn't long before I begin to hate those words – especially when it is still dark.

I wonder why I'm chosen for this when the boys are already up to help with the barn chores but I don't dare question Aunt Greta. I grudgingly throw off my covers, step on to the icy cold floor and grope my way downstairs to the stove.

Today I got two letters in the mail. One from Mama and one from Emma. I hurry to my room, flop on the bed and tear open Mama's letter first. I skim her letter and learn she, Fredrick and Hans are doing well now that there are less people to feed. With a sigh, I read Emma's slowly. She tells me how much she misses me and how hard school is this year. She hopes things are better for me in America. I set her letter down and ponder how I'll be able to tell her anything without Aunt Greta finding out. I know, I'll mail the next letter when I go to Confirmation class. Then she won't know. I sit up and feel much better because I've found a way around Aunt Greta knowing what I write to Emma.

That night I say to Margaret, "I don't see why I have to start the fire every morning when the boys are already up for the chores."

Margaret shrugs her shoulders and says, "I don't know why you have to do it. I guess Mama figures you must be able to handle it being that you're big and strong."

I shake my head and turn away so she won't see the tears in my eyes.

CHAPTER ELEVEN

"Few Bright Spots"

Life for me has few bright spots but one is Confirmation Class where I'm treated with respect and love. Pastor Schafer often asks how Gretchen and I are doing in our new home and I tell him. Gretchen is learning English much faster than I am and therefore not persecuted as much at school. However, I'm still teased mercilessly with the taunting boys mimicking how I talk.

At Confirmation Class we study many Bible verses and hymns. I've picked a favorite of each – John 3:16 is the Bible verse, "For God so loved the world that he gave his only begotten Son, that whosoever believeth in him should not perish but have everlasting life." My favorite hymn is "What a Friend We Have in Jesus." I often find myself thinking of the verses to this hymn and they help me.

Paul tries to get at me again but this time Max helps me. Max comes around the corner just as Paul starts pawing at my breasts and gives him a tongue-lashing about leaving the German girls alone. Paul leaves me alone after that. However, I worry about Gretchen because now and then she and Paul get together and whisper – just a bit too friendly.

One other person shows interest in me and Gretchen and that is Aunt Bertha, Aunt Greta's older sister. Aunt Bertha's own children are grown and gone. Occasionally she comes to visit and when she does, always asks to see us. We sit with her in the living room and visit – something that is never done with Aunt Greta. I learn that Aunt Bertha talked about sending for us long ago to Aunt Greta and was disappointed when Aunt Greta sent for us before she could. By the way Aunt Bertha looks down at her hands I can see there is more to this story than she is telling. I don't say anything but put this in the back of my mind to ask more about one day when I visit her.

As the weeks and months go slowly by, I resign myself to the hard farm life I must live. I'm not heavy but of stocky build with broad shoulders. Because of this, Aunt Greta and Uncle Alfred think I'm strong enough to work like the boys. They tell me to chop wood, carry hay bundles and lift heavy farm equipment. As I do this heavy work I become stronger and stronger. Soon I'm so fast at chopping wood that I race with the boys just for fun. We set up a stack and see who finishes first and I often win.

Throughout it all, however, I pray to God for strength to handle my life in rich America and God answers my prayers.

CHAPTER TWELVE

"Move to the City"

I am confirmed on Palm Sunday, 1924, and when I say my vows to remain faithful to the church all my life, I mean it. My love for God and all He has done for me, still does for me, gives me a solid foundation to stand on and carries me through the bad times.

When I finish eighth grade that spring, I am through with school. I can now speak English well enough so the boys stop teasing. I do break into German whenever I'm with anyone who will speak it but have now resigned myself to mostly English.

Soon I leave the farm to stay with Bertha, the Becker's oldest daughter, and her husband, Al. When I tell Gretchen I'm leaving, she shrugs her shoulders and says, "I figured you wouldn't be staying long. Seems all the older girls go off somewhere. Suppose I will when I get older too."

When I hug her, she stiffens and moves away. I'm not sure if she's happy or sad to see me leave.

I tell her, "I'll be seeing you, you know. Probably on Sunday, when everybody comes home for dinner. Be good."

The Ginnows live in Neenah and have two boys, Kenneth age four and Raymond age two. I help take care of the boys and do most of the housework.

Times are hard and money scarce. The Ginnows make it clear to me that I am an extra mouth to feed. Here too, I can never eat all I want at any meal. I get small portions only and often feel hungry at night. Sometimes I sneak food from the kitchen. If there is some cake left in the pan on the cupboard, I cut a ¼" slice all across it so nobody knows any was taken. I vow one day to be able to eat all I want.

Kenneth and Raymond are a delight and I love taking care of them. I stay with the Ginnows a year but also work certain days at Johnson's Shoe Factory in Neenah. Here I find the men loud and rough. When the foreman isn't looking, they often push us women around and sometimes try to touch our breasts. When I tell Uncle Alfred about this, he tells me to quit the job at the factory and stay with the Ginnows so I do.

One afternoon I stop to see Aunt Bertha. She greets me warmly and takes me to her living room where we sit and talk.

"How do you like living with the Ginnows, Heidi?" she asks.

"Oh, fine. I love taking care of the boys and Bertha and Al are good to me."

"I'm so glad because I know how your Aunt Greta can be."

Then she folds her hands and sits up a bit straighter. The way she is hesitating, I figure she has something important to tell me and it is. She tells me how jealous Aunt Greta is of everyone, especially her.

She begins, "I talked about sending for you girls several months before she did and as soon as I mentioned it, she must have run home and written a letter to your mother. She had to have because about the time I was to mail my letter to your mother, she came running over one day shaking a letter in my face and saying, 'I'm getting the girls. I'm getting the girls.' Of course then I never mailed my letter."

Aunt Bertha then told me several sad stories about Aunt Greta, what a gossip she is and how people avoid her whenever they can.

I don't say anything. Just listen. But I can see the pain in Aunt Bertha's eyes. I can feel her pain because I suffered much when I lived with Aunt Greta.

After that day, I stop in to see Aunt Bertha often and we become great friends.

CHAPTER THIRTEEN

"The Clark's"

On my sixteenth birthday, Margaret asks, "How'd you like to come live with me and work for the C. B. Clark's in Neenah? They need another maid and I told them about you."

"Oh, could I?"

The Clarks are wealthy. They are part-owners with the Kimberlys of the Kimberly-Clark Corporation, a large papermaking company with home offices in Neenah, Wisconsin, and several plants in the South and East. Margaret's work is in the kitchen. I would be the general maid who waits on table at meal time and do light housekeeping.

The Clarks hire me and I love working for them. I have my own large room with windows that look out on their beautiful front lawn. The walls are papered with yellow and light blue flowers. Large fluffy white curtains cover the window. I'm back to a goose down bed and feel like I've died and gone to heaven. I pray, "Thank you, dear God for blessing me with this chance. Oh thank you, thank you."

The Clark's are so good to me and I'm happier here than I've been since coming to America. I can eat all I want at meal time. They have a grand piano in the living room. When I dust it, I sit on the bench and pretend I'm playing. One day Mrs. Clark catches me sitting there and says, "Go ahead and play it, Heidi. Any time you want. We don't hear it like we used to when our daughter was young."

"Oh, no," I say. "I can't but I wish I could."

"If you like it, you should take lessons one day,"

"Maybe some day."

That day I receive a letter from Mama who tells me she's ill and seeing a physician. She can't stop coughing and sometimes almost passes out from it. I fold the letter and out of concern for her, pray that God will help her get well.

One Saturday Margaret races up the steps and bursts into my room saying, "The circus is coming to town this weekend. Let's go and have some fun."

We eagerly go to the event and among the brightly-colored booths see one of a fortune-teller.

"Oh, let's go see what's in our future," says Margaret, her dark eyes shining with excitement.

"Why not."

We enter the booth in great anticipation and I'm first. The lady is dressed in a filmy blue gown. She studies my hand by twisting and turning it over and back. She runs her finger across the lines in the palm of my hand and then closes her eyes. After a spellbinding few minutes she says, "You will marry a man with red hair. You will have four children, two boys and two girls. A dark-haired woman will give you much grief. Your homeland is Germany but you will never return there. You will never see your family in Germany again."

I feel a bit sad about her mention of my family in Germany but smile at the red-haired husband. I've never even met a man with red hair.

Margaret eagerly tells me what the fortune-teller told her – how she will marry a well-to-do merchant and have two children. She's so excited about her news, she never asks what I was told but that's OK because I really don't want to tell her. As superstitious as my grandmothers and Mama had been, I'm not so sure about all this. Actually I hope she's wrong.

CHAPTER FOURTEEN

"Dan"

One day Margaret rushes into my room and breathlessly tells me, "Heidi! I met this boy. His name is Harry and he works in the meat department at Kroger's Corner Store. He wants to take me to the movies Saturday night."

"How nice," I say.

Soon Harry regularly comes to see Margaret and they often ask me along when they go dancing. I go a few times but feel like they'd rather be alone so I say "no" the next time they ask.

One day Margaret says, "How'd you like to go on a blind date next Saturday?"

"What's that?"

"It's when you go out with someone you've never met. Harry has this friend, Dan, and he's looking for a date for him."

"Well, what if I don't like him? What if we don't get along?"

"Then you don't see him again, Silly. Come on. Harry and I will be right there. No need to worry. Two couples out dancing. It'll be fun. What do you think?"

"I'll think about it. What's he like anyway?"

"Well, Harry likes him and that's something. He's tall and has red hair."

"Red hair! Are you kidding?" I immediately remember what the fortune-teller told me.

"Nope. It's carrot-top red."

After thinking about this a few minutes, I decide I might like to meet this redhead.

I change my clothes three times for this blind date. Why I care so much is beyond me but for some reason it's important to look my very best for this redhead.

My heart is in my throat when the boys drive up in a 1920 black Ford coupe. My wobbly legs manage to take me down to the car behind Margaret. Margaret gets in the front, I am motioned to the back. I get in and face this redhead, Dan. And my heart stops. He is absolutely the most handsome man I've ever seen. His red hair isn't so red, it's mainly reddish-brown. I smile when Harry says, "Heidi, this is Dan. Dan, Heidi." Dan gives me a crooked grin and we shake hands.

The evening goes by in a blur but it is a heavenly blur for me. Although we don't talk much, we do have fun dancing. I never really learned to dance very well but it didn't take me long to discover I love it. Dan seems as interested in me as I am in him and I hope to see him again.

And I do. Every Saturday night Margaret and I are ready by the time the boys say they'll be there. However, it's rare they come anywhere near that time. Both work on farms and don't always finish their work when they'd like to. We often get frustrated and throw our shoes across the room, vowing not to go out with the boys that night. But as soon as we hear the Ford drive up, we rush to retrieve those shoes and hurry down to the car entirely forgetting all our earlier frustration.

Most dates are dances at the Grange Hall. But it isn't long before Dan invites me to his family farm. One warm Sunday afternoon I meet Dan's family and see his parents place. I can't believe how huge the farm is. Dan says it's two hundred acres, much larger than the Becker farm. There are two large barns and several other buildings – all painted bright red. The house is huge and painted white with green trim. Grass is mowed around the buildings and everything looks well cared for. Dan's parents are quiet but cordial. His sisters seem shy but his brothers are just the opposite. I smile and coax them into talking. Before long we are laughing and joking. I love to have fun and find it easy to get to know people. I can tease with the best of them and Dan's family seem to welcome me with open arms.

As time goes on, Dan and I fall in love. We pick a special song we often hear at the dances called "Always." Some of the words are, "I'll be loving you, always. With a love that's true, always. Not for just an hour, not for just a day, not for just a year, but always, always." It seems to say exactly how we feel about each other.

One Sunday Dan and I go to the Becker's farm so he can meet Aunt Greta and Uncle Alfred. My stomach is filled with butterflies because I so want them to like him. Actually I shouldn't care if they do or not but somehow I do. There was no need to worry, however, because as soon as Uncle Alfred finds out Dan is a farmer and plans to have his own some day, he smiles broadly and avidly shakes his hand.

CHAPTER FIFTEEN

"Our Own Place"

February 14, 1929, Dan and I marry in a double wedding with Harry and Margaret. The ceremony is held at the pastor's home in the living room with only immediate family present. After the ceremony, pictures are taken and we go out to dinner at the Valley Inn.

Hildegarde Augusta Matilda Tesch and
Daniel Benjamin Romberg
Married February 14, 1929

We move in with Dan's parents until we get a place of our own.

A month after our marriage, I receive a letter from Aunt Belle in Germany. Assuming it is congratulating me on my marriage, I quickly tear the envelope open and eagerly begin to read.

The news hits me in the stomach and I have to sit down on the nearest chair. Mama has died of tuberculosis. She'd been placed in a sanitarium but only lasted a few months. Enclosed in the letter is a picture of her in a white dress laying in her casket.

I slowly lower the letter to my lap and stare at the picture. How young she looks. How peaceful. No tears come as I stare at Mama. Only bad memories of her meanness flood over me. Fritz is almost eighteen now and Hans nearly fourteen. I wonder what will happen to them? Fritz had talked about military school. Maybe he is there already. But Hans would be too young for that. Or would he?

One day Dan takes me to see a place he is hoping to buy with help from his father. The driveway is a quarter mile down the road from Dan's home place and a mile longer to the buildings. When we get to the house, I see goats looking out the upstairs windows, chewing delightfully on something that looks like straw.

The buildings are rundown and in need of much repair and paint. In the house, I start to walk across the kitchen floor to the next room when Dan grabs my arm and stops me.

"Don't walk there. The floor is ready to fall into the basement. I have to rebuild it."

We walk around the edge of the room to the next where the floor is solid. As I look around, I can see this being a wonderful home.

I hug and kiss him. "Oh, Dan, this will be great. When can we move in?"

"Well, that'll be a while. You see all the work that needs to be done. I'll call Harry and Bud and see if they can come on out and help me. My brothers will too. Maybe we can get started next week."

"Wonderful. That's wonderful!"

CHAPTER SIXTEEN

"A Farmer's Wife"

Buzz, buzz, buzzzzzzzzz! I keep hearing this strange buzzing sound. It's so close to me but how can it be in my bedroom at this hour? I slowly open my eyes and see a huge yellow-and-black bumblebee inches from my face. I scream and fling back the covers.

Dan stands there laughing while he holds his pliars near my face, a huge bumble bee struggles to get free.

"That sure got you up, sleepyhead. Now maybe you'll stop ignoring the alarm clock every morning and help me in the barn."

"You're mean. Know that? I'm coming. I'm coming. Now get that thing out of here before it stings somebody."

And that was the last time I ignored the alarm clock and rolled over to catch a few more minutes of sleep.

The first time I try to milk the cows, I soon learn there is a trick to it.

"I can't get anything to come out," I whine.

"Here. You have to hold the teat with your whole hand, not just your fingers. Like this," says Dan. I watch him fold his entire hand around the cow's teat and squeeze while gently pulling downward. A huge squirt of milk drains into the pail.

"You know, I can hardly sit on this stool right, say nothing about holding the teat right," I say.

"You'll get it. Now try again."

I take a good grip of the bulging teat and squeeze. The cow kicks and I fly off the stool and into the manure-filled gutter.

"Ouch! Now what'd I do wrong?"

"Let me see your fingernails," says Dan trying his hardest to hide a grin. He looks at my nails and says, "You need to cut these shorter. You're digging them into the teat and it's hurting her. You run up to the house and get cleaned up and cut those nails."

When I return with shorter fingernails, I set up the three-legged stool and try once again.

Dan says, "Another thing to keep in mind when milking cows is to talk softly to them. They let their milk down faster if you pet them a little on their hip here and talk softly to them. Sometimes I hum while I'm milking and they seem to like that too."

I sit down and try again. This time when I squeeze and gently pull downward, a small stream of milk drips out of the teat. I feel elated. I try again. This time more comes and I keep working until my hand aches. Then I try to do what I'd seen Dan do – use both hands on the two back teats of the cow. It works and my milking technique improves. Before long, I keep up with Dan in getting all the milk from the cow's udder.

Something is going on in the workshop. Think I'll go see what it might be. Dan seems to go down there quite often and always shuts the door. When I open the door, Plow Boy tobacco wrappers lay all over the floor and Dan's face turns bright red. I put my hands on my hips and say, "So. A little tobacco-chewing going on behind my back, huh?"

"I—err—was—I was going to tell you but – "

"I already knew long ago, Dan. You can't hide something like that from anyone for very long. I knew back when we were dating that you chewed. Just wish you'd told me before I caught you. Learned anything here?"

I hug him and he sighs with relief.

Dan and I proudly own, on halves with his Dad, one hundred sixty acres of land, eight cows, two goats and four horses. We milk the cows every morning and night. Seven of our cows are giving good amounts of milk each time. One cow isn't coming along as well. Three of our cows will have calves in several months.

The last few mornings my stomach has been upset. I find myself running for the sink. First thought is maybe the cows aren't the only pregnant ones. I beam with the possibility that I, too, might have a baby soon.

If I hadn't learned much about farming so far, this much I did know. There is always work to be done. Not only do we have the milking twice a day, but we have to think about our crops. With the calves arrival, we need to prepare pens where the mothers can be with their babies a while before going back to the herd.

Me and two calves

Dan wants to buy pigs and chickens just as soon as we have the money and that will mean more work. Won't be long and we're going to need to hire someone to help us.

CHAPTER SEVENTEEN

"Old Mr. Grump"

One fine summer day I hear Dan yelling from the barnyard. I drop the water pail I'm carrying to the chicken coop and run to see what's wrong. When I get to the barn, I see Dan circling the haystack as fast as he can run with our billy goat, Mr. Grump, tight behind. As Dan comes to the side of the stack nearest the door, I yell, "Once more around," and laugh. The look of dismay on his face makes me feel a bit guilty but the way he's frantically running is hilarious and I want to see him do it once more.

On his next trip around I quickly open the door and he makes a mad dash for it. I slam the door shut just as Mr. Grump rams his four-inch horns into it. Dan is huffing and puffing and leans over his knees trying to catch his breath.

"OK, you," he pants. "Why didn't you op-open that door ri-right away?"

"Oh, I was having too much fun watching you run. You sure can when you have to can't you?"

And then I laugh again at his narrow escape.

I wasn't too surprised the next Monday when Old Mr. Grump was loaded on Pa Romberg's truck for a trip to the Milwaukee stock yard. Dan had had enough narrow escapes being chased by him. And I lost some good entertainment.

CHAPTER EIGHTEEN

"Our Son, Harvey"

April 27, 1930, during a wild spring storm complete with thunder and lightning, Dan drives me to the hospital. Four hours later, our firstborn son enters the world. I want to name him Daniel but Dan wants his name to be Harvey. Daniel was alright with him for a second name so he is Harvey Daniel.

As I hold my baby son for the first time, my heart swells with love and pride. He's so perfect – round face, chubby cheeks, big blue eyes and all ten fingers and toes. My love for this little person makes me vow to always love and care for him. I want him to know that he's loved because the years I was growing up, I never felt loved by my mother. My father loved me, that I knew but not my mother. I never want this child to feel the way I did – ever.

During the night the electricity goes off and I lay in my bed petrified because I'm separated from my baby. I get out of bed, pull my skimpy hospital gown around me and grope along the wall to the door. The strong odor of antiseptics hurts my nose as I enter the hall. Before I can take a step, a nurse comes and asks, "What can I do for you?" I tell her I want my baby and she says, "Oh, no. That's not possible. Feeding time isn't until 2:00 a.m. Go back to bed. We'll bring him to you then."

I slowly turn around and just as I reach my door, the lights come back on. Under my breath I say, "Never again am I having a baby in the hospital. If I'm privileged to have any more, I'll have them at home and know where my little one is at all times."

With Harvey to care for, we desperately need to hire someone to help with the work and so we hire Mark, a neighbor boy. He is eighteen and the oldest of four sons. He comes to live with us and soon becomes part of the family.

Even though I now have a baby to care for, I help milk the cows. Harvey is in a basket near the entrance to the barn and I check on him each trip to the milk house. He doesn't seem to care where he is as long as I'm nearby. When he cries, I'm just a few steps away.

My days are full with the extra work of washing diapers, the usual housework of cleaning, baking and cooking plus helping with the milking morning and night. There's never a moment when I wonder what to do.

Mark is able to help with the milking until the spring planting starts. Then he is busy planting. This means red-and-white clover mixed hay for the cattle, Timothy hay for the horses, oats and barley, field corn for silage in the silos and ear corn in the corn crib for the hogs and chickens. After the crops are planted I think the work should lessen but it doesn't. Now the corn needs to be cultivated to keep the weeds down. Mark is good with the horses and handles the cultivating with little if any instruction from Dan.

With all the necessary work on the farm there is little time for fun.

CHAPTER NINETEEN

"Pa's Teasing"

Sunday mornings are hectic with milking the cows, breakfast and getting ready for church. We hurry through as fast as we can and hop in our Model A Ford and drive the ten miles to Winneconne. Church is a place of peace. Today we're singing my favorite hymn, "What a Friend We Have in Jesus." What a lucky day. We enjoy worshiping our God and talking to other members of the congregation.

Sundays are also time for visiting family. We see Ma and Pa Romberg one Sunday, Gretchen, Aunt Greta and Uncle Albert the next. Sometimes we stop in to see Margaret and Harry. They don't have any children yet so still go dancing and to the movies. Dan and I are so busy with farm work we rarely find time for such things.

Visiting relatives and friends is a real highlight to our lives though. But it has it's anxious moments too. At the Romberg's, Pa teases me, "Oh, I'll bet that baby of yours isn't a boy. Looks like a girl to me."

I get weary of his teasing and end it one Sunday when I say, "OK. You want to change his dirty diaper next time and find out for yourself that he's a boy?"

Pa laughs and that's the last time he teases me about Harvey being a girl.

We often see Dan's married brothers and sisters at Ma and Pa's. His brother Kimball has a girl and it seems when she fusses, everybody gets up to care for her. My Harvey cries and cries and nobody seems to care. I sure feel bad about it but try not to let it bother me.

CHAPTER TWENTY

"Our Son, Leslie"

Our second son, Leslie William, is born May 26, 1933. We call him Leslie because we like the name and William after Dan's father. This time my baby is born at home where I know he is safe. As with Harvey, my heart swells with love and pride. This little one is perfect too – just like his older brother. How blessed I feel with two lovely sons. Harvey is three years old and so excited to have a little brother that he is not jealous of him in the least. Between babies I've gained a lot of weight. The doctor doesn't seem to care. Dan doesn't care, so I don't either. Food tastes so good to me now that I can have all I want. I'm afraid I love to eat too much. Instead of weighing 110 pounds, I now weigh 180 pounds.

One evening after supper I have a sharp pain under my left breast. I lie down and try hard to hold my breath, hoping it will go away. Soon it does and I sigh with relief.

A couple days later I have the same thing only this time more sharp, knife-like. This time the pain lasts longer. Although it's hard to ignore this, I keep hoping it will all go away and stay away.

It doesn't. After several attacks I see Dr. Phillips. He examines me and tells me if they keep coming, I will need surgery for gall bladder disease.

The next week I have a terrible attack which lasts and lasts. I'm in such pain I don't care if they do the surgery on my kitchen table. Dan calls Dr. Phillips out to the house and by the time he arrives I'm lying in bed twisting and turning in agony. I pray for God to help me and beg Dr. Phillips to do something. I'm rushed to the hospital for surgery on my gall bladder.

I don't remember much the next few days but at the age of only twenty-three, I have my gall bladder removed. My name is written in the medical journals for I am the second youngest in the United States of America to have that done.

My stay in the hospital is memorable because at one time I am sure I'm close to death. I see Jesus standing over me. He is wearing a white robe and rays of sunlight beam around him. He smiles at me and I have the strongest feeling I'm going to be alright.

After that vision, I begin to recover. There is a tube sticking out of my incision and ugly bile-type liquid drains from it. I am in the hospital three weeks and in such agony most of that time I didn't care if I live or die until that vision of Jesus.

Ma Romberg comes to take care of the boys. Leslie just started walking when I went to the hospital. Ma put him in a walker and he had to learn to walk all over again.

It is many weeks before I totally recover from the surgery but finally am able to take care of the boys, Dan and my house again.

CHAPTER TWENTY ONE

"Walking in a Storm"

Winter is harsh on the farm. When the animals are kept inside the barn all day and night, there is much more work keeping them watered, fed and clean. Mark is a big help with the milking and cleaning the barn every day. With two little ones, I can't help out there anymore. I have too much to do with the boys and the house. Even though it's bitter cold, I wash clothes every Monday and hang them out on the line. They freeze before drying so they are stiff as a board when I bring them in. I hang them around the house to dry.

Difficult as winter is, I do love the snow and the cold. When I dress warm, I'm fine. And when we have a blizzard, I love to take a walk in it, down the road or the back lane. There is something about the blowing and wildness that inspires me. Often I sing my favorite "What a Friend We Have in Jesus" at the top of my lungs. I am always careful I don't lose my way and make sure I don't overdo. When it's winter, I often think back of summer and how I love a good rain storm. I walk in that too, but never a thunder storm, only lots of wind and rain.

One wintry storm, I scare Dan. When I come into the house he walks over to me and hugs me saying, "Where have you been? Don't you know there's a blizzard going on out there? You could have gotten lost."

"Oh Dan, no. I won't get lost. I just love the wildness of the storm and never go far." Then I hug him for his concern.

Mark laughs at us and sits down to take his shoes and socks off. Then he cleans his toes with his fingers. After that he walks over to the cupboard and cuts himself a huge piece of chocolate cake and eats it. I nearly gag when I think how dirty his hands are from playing with his feet but say nothing.

CHAPTER TWENTY TWO

"Gretchen"

"Gretchen is seeing someone we really don't like, Heidi. Can she come stay with you and Dan for a while?"

It was Bertha. Gretchen now stays with her in Neenah and helps with the housework and care of the boys much like I had done earlier.

At age nineteen, Gretchen has her own ideas on who to see and when. At this age I can see where this could mean trouble. I wonder how she'd be had we stayed in Germany? And again, although I'm so much happier since marrying Dan, I still wonder why it is that we are in America?

"Sure. Why don't I stop and pick her up tomorrow after I get groceries."

"Sounds good. I'll have her pack a suitcase and tell her it's only for a while."

When I pick Gretchen up, she gets in the car, slams the door and slouches down in her seat. She folds her arms across her tight-fitting white blouse, a frown on her face and her lower lip sticking out.

"Tweet, tweet, tweet," I say and with two fingers flapping back and forth like a bird I reach over to "land" on her lower lip. She shakes her head and tries not to smile at the silly joke but her lower lip returns to normal.

I laugh and say, "You got the message. If a bird can sit on that lip, it must really stick out and you're really pouting about something. What's the matter?"

She unfolds her arms and sits up straight, her green eyes burning with anger.

"If Bertha thinks I'm done with Sam she's got another thing coming. We love each other and nothing's keeping us apart for long. He'll wait 'til I'm back. You'll see."

"Oh. I see. You think this guy is it, huh?"

"Yeah. He is and don't start in on 'you're too young' with me," she said in a sing-song manner. "I'm sick of people telling me that."

"Don't you want the guy who's 'it' to be liked by people who care about you? Don't you care what we all think?"

"Oh, never mind. You don't understand."

Gretchen slouches down in the seat again and looks out the window.

Gretchen helps out around the house and with the outside work and seems to settle down. Once in a while she asks to use the phone but never stays on it very long so I became suspicious that her great love wasn't missing her as much as she misses him.

Then one evening when I come around the corner of the milk house, I catch her standing next to Dan, her arm around his waist, her face close to his as she stares intently up at him.

When she sees me, she quickly moves away and turns her back on me. I frown and think, "What's that rascal up to?"

In the rush of getting the chores done, I forget the incident.

A couple nights later, Dan goes out to work in his shop. Soon I notice Gretchen sneak along the side of the shop and looking both ways, open the door and go in.

I wait a few minutes and then boldly go down to the shop and open the door. Gretchen stands next to Dan with her arms around his neck. Dan stiffens and leans back.

"Alright, Gretchen. You're going back to Bertha's tomorrow. Get in the house and pack your bags, now."

Gretchen slinks out of the shop and goes up to the house. I look at Dan. He shrugs his shoulders, looks me right in the eye and says, "I wanted nothing to do with her. I'm glad she's getting out of here."

CHAPTER TWENTY THREE

"Money Trouble"

Dan and I don't fight very often but when we do, ninety percent of the time it's over money. We agree on most things because I usually give in to whatever he wants. I know most of our income has to go back into the farm so we can keep growing but there has to be some income for what I need in the house.

One day I say, "Dan, look at that couch. It's falling apart. We really need a new one."

"We can't be wasting money on a new couch. It's going to have to wait," Dan says his eyes glaring, hands in fists at his sides.

"Wait! That's all you ever say. And it isn't only the couch. The boys and I need winter coats. You tell me I should wear last years. Well, maybe I can but the boys can't. They've outgrown them. Harvey's from last year is worn out so Leslie can't wear it They both need stuff besides that."

"Oh, come on. Things will get better when the money comes in from the clover seed. We'll talk about this more then."

Dan walks out of the kitchen and leaves me standing there, the list I'd given him tossed on the table. I stomp my foot and bite my lip. Even though tears try to come, I won't let them. I force myself to let it go.

So, again, I'm told to wait – wait – wait while anything he needs outside is bought. Like the new McCormick Deering tractor. He and his brother Ed each bought one so they did get a good deal. But again, no problem for what he wants. The boys and I need clothes. I sew what I can but there are times we need things I can't make. I've had it with this problem.

That next afternoon, still steaming over the argument, I stop to see Aunt Bertha. How I adore this plump little lady in her spotless flowered apron. The minute she sees me she says "Oh, oh. Something's wrong. You're not smiling today. What is it?"

"Oh, Aunt Bertha, Dan and I had another terrible fight over money. I need things in the house, the boys need clothes, I need clothes but that doesn't count. Whatever he needs or wants outside we get. I'm told to wait. What am I going to do?"

"Well," Aunt Bertha says and she puts her arm around my shoulder, "First of all you come sit down and I'll put a pot of coffee on. I just made some banana bread so we'll have a slice or two of that with it. Then we'll get to your problem."

Having blurted out my troubles to someone who cares about me helps in itself. The coffee and treat are also calming. After my second cup of coffee I begin again, "Dan doesn't seem to care if I wear the same old housedress to church every Sunday or when we go anywhere. He doesn't care that the boys' clothes are looking drab or shorter than they should because they've outgrown them. I'm tired of patching things again and again when to me we have the money for what we need. He just ignores our needs. He's wonderful in so many ways, a fabulous farmer, works hard but yet - - "

"Heidi, a man is responsible for his wife and family. You need to get a charge account at Sears or Penneys or some department store you regularly shop at and charge the things you need. Don't go off the deep end, mind you, but when you or the boys need something, you get it, charge it to Dan and he will get the bill in the mail. There's nothing he can do about it but pay it. And if he fights you on this, you tell him you're only charging necessities."

On the way home I whistle a happy tune because I've found an answer to this nightmare I'd been living. Now all I have to do is weather the storm that first bill will bring.

CHAPTER TWENTY FOUR

"The Accusation"

One day the phone rings. It's Margaret.

"If you think you're getting away with it you have another guess coming."

"What?"

"My picture. The one you took from my buffet yesterday. You're the only one who could have taken it because it was there before you came and now it's missing. Well? What do you have to say?"

"First of all I didn't take anything. Second of all, what in heaven's name picture are you talking about?"

"Our wedding picture. The one of you and Dan and me and Harry. What a mistake having a double wedding with the likes of you. Now bring my picture back."

"But, Margaret – " was all I got out when she slams the receiver down and the line goes dead.

I slowly hang the receiver up and close my mouth. My mind races back to yesterday when the boys and I stopped at her place for a short visit. I've done that a lot on my grocery shopping trips. She's done the same when she is over my way. Where would she get such a ridiculous idea that I'd take anything? Didn't all these years of friendship mean anything?

I shake my head and stare out the window. I know which wedding picture she's talking about but we have our own. Why would I want hers? The more I think about it the more insane it becomes.

"Take her picture, indeed," I whisper to myself and go out to check the wash.

As I'm taking down the dry wash I'm thinking about that conversation with Margaret. We've always been best friends but is this any way to treat a "best friend?"

So what do I do with this accusation, let it go a few days? Maybe she's just having a bad day and took her frustration out on me.

Do I call her back? Go over there? What a mess. Wonder what really happened to her picture? Could one of the boys have picked it up and put it someplace else?

When the boys come in for lunch, I show them the picture and ask, "Did you see this at Aunt Margaret's house yesterday?"

Both boys look at it and shake their heads.

"We never went in the house. Just stayed out in the yard and played with those kittens by the porch," says Harvey.

Then I remembered. The boys hadn't gone into the house.

"Go eat your lunch, boys. Mommy's going to call Aunt Margaret."

But as soon as Margaret knows it is me, she slams the receiver down and I feel hurt and frustrated.

The next Sunday dinner at Aunt Greta's we avoid each other. When I come anywhere near her, she walks away. Harry and Dan treat each other as usual, talking about their jobs and old times. Margaret glares at Harry often but he just ignores her.

When we get home, I ask, "Dan, did you notice how Margaret avoided me today?"

"It wasn't real noticeable in the crowd but now that you mention it, she was rather cool to me too."

"What should I do? I've tried calling, she hangs up. I'm sure if I went over she'd slam the door in my face."

"You two must have had problems before, how'd you settle them then?'

"Yes, we have. She's the most stubborn, self-centered person I know and yet we've had a lot of fun too. When I really think about it, seems like she comes around after a while but this is different. She's accusing me of stealing from her and I never did. Really makes me mad."

"Well, let's give her some time. Maybe she'll find it somewhere and this will all be nothing but a bad memory. Got anything good to eat?"

The words of the fortune teller Margaret and I saw years ago comes to mind. "I'd have much trouble from a dark-haired woman." Margaret has dark brown hair. Could she have meant her? Could she have meant this? Well, if so, I sure am having trouble from that dark-haired woman all right.

A verse of my favorite hymn, "What a Friend we have in Jesus" runs through my mind. "Do thy friends despise, forsake thee? Take it to the Lord in prayer. In his arms he'll take and shield thee. Thou wilt find a solace there." I pray, Dear Jesus, please help me with this mess. Please!

Summer ends, fall comes and goes. Soon it is Christmas. With the hustle and bustle of preparations and shopping, I forget about the trouble with Margaret. Although we two couples have always exchanged gifts and spent time together over the holidays, there would be none of that this year.

Then one day the phone rings. It is Margaret. With a very meek voice which I could hardly hear, she says," I - - I - - I'm so- - sorry, Heidi.

All this time I was so sure you'd taken our wedding picture but now I know you didn't."

"And how is this?"

"Well – this afternoon Harry and I decided to put up the Christmas tree and when we moved the buffet, the picture fell out from behind it. It was stuck on the small ledge in the back of the buffet. Can you forgive an old German fool?"

"Course, you old crow! Now when are you guys coming over to see our tree?"

When Margaret, Harry and their son Bobby came over, we hug as if nothing has happened while I silently pray, "Thank you, Dear God. Thank you."

CHAPTER TWENTY FIVE

"Harvey Starts School"

"I know he's only five years old but we've decided he should start first grade now. We'll need his help on the farm as he grows up and if he starts early, he'll finish early. You see we want him to go farther than his Dad or me. We only went through eighth grade. At seventeen and graduated from high school he'll be more help on the farm."

"Well," drawls the school teacher, "Alright but he will have to prove he's ready by handling his assignments."

All day I think about my Harvey being old enough for school. How I miss him. How wonderful to have Leslie to care for. Much as I want my boys educated, I still want to keep them near me where I know they're safe.

Harvey walks the mile and a half to Town Line School. His father and grandfather attended this same school so the Romberg name is well known there. Harvey likes school and seems to do well with his studies. Leslie misses him as much or maybe more than I do and runs to meet him every day when he sees him coming up the road.

One thing I'm most interested in is the movies. Clark Gable, Greta Garbo, Claudette Colbert, Gary Cooper and little Shirley Temple are some of my favorites. How I loved "It Happened One Night" with Clark Gable and Claudette Colbert. Sometimes when I'm off shopping, I'll take in a movie and make sure I see anything Shirley Temple is in. I find myself often dreaming about life as seen in the movies and when I try to tell Dan about this, he scoffs at me saying, "Oh, sure you wish things were like they are in the movies. You know that's all fairy tale stuff don't you? Life isn't anything like the movies, Heidi, believe me."

"Well, maybe not everything," I say, "But dancing is real. We used to go all the time. We never do anymore and I miss it. Don't you?"

"Sometimes, but if we don't take care of our business here on the farm, we won't make it. You know how much work there always is. But that doesn't mean we never go to the movies. When that western comes out you talked about with Gary Cooper, let me know. We'll see that we get to that one."

When the western comes out, we go. So, I don't go to the movies alone or with the boys all the time – just most of the time.

CHAPTER TWENTY SIX

"Pa Dies"

Dan hangs up the phone and says, "Pa's had a bad fall. I have to run home," and he hurries out the door. I grab Harvey and Leslie as they try to follow Dan and tell them, "No, boys you can't go along. Daddy's in a hurry and needs to help Grandpa."

I try to go about my chores as usual but can't help but think about what could have happened and silently pray he's going to be alright.

When Dan gets back home hours later, near chore time, he looks ashen. "Is he going to be alright? What happened?"

"He told Elmer and Bill to go up in the haymow and throw hay down for the cows and they didn't do it. So, he went up there. He slipped on something and fell all the way to the floor. He's gone, Heidi. Gone."

I hug Dan and putting my head on his shoulder feel the tears forming in my eyes. Pa Romberg had always been good to me even though he'd get to teasing too much sometimes. I couldn't believe he was gone.

"The undertaker came just as I was leaving so Ma will be calling about the arrangements. Funeral will probably be Friday I'd guess."

Wiping his eyes with his farmer's red handkerchief, he says, "Best get out to the barn."

The funeral home Thursday night is jammed with family and friends. I stay with the boys until their bedtime and then take them home. Dan stays with his Ma and Elmer brings him home afterwards.

The day of the funeral is a beautiful, spring day. On such a day, it's hard to believe Dan's father will soon be buried. The service goes well until the sermon when Pastor Schultz says some very negative things about Pa, how he really wasn't much of a church-goer but was now accounting for this to his Maker. Try as I could, I couldn't help but feel the man was preaching like Pa wasn't in heaven and that just couldn't be. Pa talked about his faith on occasion. I left the service upset.

It was a long day dealing with all the people, trying to keep an eye on the boys as they ran with their cousins and mulling over and over in my mind what Pastor meant by some of the things he said.

When we get home I say to Dan, "What did you think of Pastor's sermon? Don't you think he said some rather bad things about Pa?"

"Well, maybe what he had to say was just how he felt about him. God alone knows what was in Pa's heart and that's what I'm going to remember, not some sermon given by some man."

Weeks pass and every Sunday when I listen to Pastor Schultz, I can't help but hear the negative things he said about Pa. Dan's Ma and sisters have mentioned their feelings to me and seem to feel the same way about what happened at Pa's funeral. Sometimes I think we should leave St. Paul's and change our membership to Grace in Winchester. But when I talk to Dan about this, he shakes his head and says, "We're not changing churches over anything that happened at Pa's funeral. We're staying right where we are because I believe St. Paul's preaches the truth. So forget Grace in Winchester."

CHAPTER TWENTY SEVEN

"Gretchen Marries"

One fall evening, Gretchen and Sam drive into our yard. I'm just finishing feeding the chickens and try to wipe my apron clean.

Gretchen runs over to me, her green eyes shining with happiness. She throws her arms around me and says, "Sam and I just got married. I wanted you to know first."

My mouth drops as I look from her happy face to his beaming smile. I hug them both and say, "My, oh my, now that is a surprise. Congratulations! Tell me all about it."

Gretchen begins her story about eloping two weeks before and how she didn't tell anyone what she was doing. She left a note for Bertha saying she'd be away a few days and not to worry. She would be fine.

Although I'm not so keen on her choice in Sam for a husband, he does appear to love her. He doesn't have much of a job at the moment but has applied at the mill in Neenah.

"I'm sure I'll get something soon," he says with a grin.

I smile and say, "Well, come on in and sit down. I'll get the coffee on and we'll have a piece of the apple pie I just took out of the oven an hour ago. Dan will be in from plowing soon. He'll want to congratulate you too."

And so, Gretchen settles down. Especially after their first daughter Pamela is born. Sam does get a job at the foundry doing shift work and they seem to get on well enough.

CHAPTER TWENTY EIGHT

"Our Daughter, Shirley"

May 19, 1937, our daughter is born. Because of my love for Shirley Temple, we name her Shirley. Being born in May means an easy second name and we call her Shirley Mae – spelled the German way. Harvey accepts his little sister immediately but Leslie hangs back when I hold her. The second time he sees her, I reach out my free arm to him and he runs to me – all smiles. From then on he must have figured his mama had one arm left for him and he's no longer jealous of her.

The news on the radio one night startles me. Germany is marching across Europe and seems unstoppable. I remember Frederick's last letter and how excited he was about this great new leader, Hitler. Maybe it is time to bring them to America. Emma's last letter is not filled with the excitement Frederick seems to have. She sounds scared and afraid to even tell me much of what is really going on. She even hints her letters may be opened.

Then it hits me hard about why Gretchen and I were sent to America. We are spared the turmoil going on in Germany. Where would we be had we stayed there? Would I be married to a German soldier who'd now be off to the war? How thankful I am to be here.

That night when Dan and I lay talking in bed, I say, "I'm worried about my brothers. Fredrick is mixed up in the military and his last letter has him thinking what's going on over there is wonderful. I don't think it is, do you?"

"No, it isn't. I'm afraid there will be lots of trouble over that Hitler. What are you thinking?"

"Do you think we could send for Fritz and Hans?"

"Maybe, but you know it's going to cost us. Yet we sure could use their help with the work."

"I'll stop and see Aunt Bertha tomorrow and find out what to do. She knows all about what it takes to send for relatives over there because she wanted to send for me and Gretchen."

We scrape together the one hundred eighty dollars it costs to send for the boys and I send it in a letter to Frederick. Several weeks later I receive his answer. Neither he nor Hans want to come to America. To them, Germany is going to be a paradise once Hitler rules. The people will have the consideration they never had before. There will be no more poverty because everyone will be treated equally. Once they get rid of all the Jews who are dragging the good German people down, things will be much better. Frederick also proudly announces he will soon join the military.

I shake my head in sorrow because my brothers have fallen for the propaganda Hitler has spread throughout Germany. I am disappointed they don't want to come. I'm also disappointed they didn't return the money.

CHAPTER TWENTY NINE

"Harvest Time"

When the beets are ripe for harvesting Dan hires migrant workers through the buyer to help at harvest time. He builds a shack at the first turn down the driveway, about one quarter mile away. Mexican families move in and live there until the harvesting is finished. The boys love to play with the Mexican children and sometimes go to the beet shack. Now and then the Mexican children come to our house.

At night the Mexicans play lively music which is carried by the wind to our house. We often sit out on the back porch and listen to their happy singing. When the migrant workers leave, the boys miss their playmates but soon they go back to playing by themselves.

End of summer also means threshing time. For three days I prepare noon meals for ten to twelve men. Dan's Case 36-inch cylinder threshing machine is the largest in the area and is powered by a 2236 McCormick Deering tractor. When he finishes our grain, he hires out to several neighbors. Everyone helps at everyone's place which is why the extra men for the noon meal. When the rig starts up there is a steady hum all day long.

I start two or three days in advance by baking pies, cakes and bread. This helps ease the load when it's time to prepare the meal. Each day I concentrate on meat, potatoes, vegetable and dessert. Often the wives of the men will help too and when peeling potatoes for my largest kettle, that extra help is really appreciated.

A typical meal is an 8 lb. beef roast, mashed potatoes and gravy, four cans of corn, two loaves of bread and two cakes. Men who work hard all morning in the fields need much food to keep up their strength.

It is well known that the men don't only stare at their plates while in the house. They look over the entire room. If they see a mess anywhere it is noted and discussed with each other and they are more than happy to tell their wives. Soon the whole neighborhood knows what a housekeeper you are. If the sewing machine has dust all over it, they will describe it in detail. So, I dust and clean everything not only in the kitchen but dining room where the meal is served.

The men don't only spread poor housekeeping around, they tell what looks good too and the taste of the meal is not forgotten either.

Every year when I prepare for this busy harvesting time, I think back to the time my chocolate cake didn't turn out and I had to tell the men "no dessert today." I was teased about that for years because dessert is as essential as meat and potatoes to a threshing crew.

I also remember the time I dropped the meat platter on the table spilling the cut up roast all over. I can still hear old Charlie Drews exclaim with a huge grin, "Ah, that's OK. Just slide the pieces back on the plate and pass it over here. Table's clean enough. Get a towel and dab up the juice a bit and forget about it. Looks great!"

When the three days of threshing end, it's awfully quiet without the hum of the big machine. Now it's Ida's turn to cook for the crew and I'll be heading over tomorrow morning to help her peel potatoes like she helped me.

Harvey and Leslie bringing in a load of hay

Threshing machine

Dan picking corn in a muddy field

CHAPTER THIRTY

"Our Daughter, Carol"

When deer hunting season comes in November, Dan takes the week of Thanksgiving off to hunt with his friends. I'm not happy about this at all because I worry about him and it puts me in charge of the hired help to take care of everything on the farm.

The fall work of picking corn and plowing are finished so the only regular work is milking morning and night plus any problems that arise like pipes freezing. It hurts me to know he doesn't care how I feel about this. So, when the time comes, I foolishly whine and complain about his being gone only to find it falls on deaf ears. I threaten to hide his rifle and his hunting clothes. He just laughs and says he'll buy new things if I do that.

1939, however, I think things will surely be different because I'm pregnant, due mid-November. All I have to do is be late in my delivery and he'll have to stay home once. But Carol Hildegarde is born November 15th – plenty early enough for him to go on his annual hunting trip.

Over the years I learned his hunting trip was a great time to do whatever I wanted to around the house. Sometimes I'd call my friends and we'd repaper the dining room or a bedroom. If I thought we needed any furniture I'd wait until he was gone to buy it. He could do nothing about it when he walked into the living room and saw a new couch or chair.

The most drastic thing I ever did was to have the two small downstairs bedrooms made into one large bedroom. I hired men to come in and take out the wall, put a closet at one end and close up one of the doors. When Dan came home that year he was quite surprised to walk into a wall instead of the door to our bedroom.

But we all missed Dan most on Thanksgiving Day. We would set a place for him at the table in the hopes he'd be there. We'd watch for him out the window but he never came home for that special day. When he did get home, he'd talk about his Thanksgiving dinner being a cold beef sandwich eaten on a stump in the woods as he watched for a deer to come by.

Dan often brought a deer home. We'd have venison steak and make some into hamburger. Any deer with many points was mounted and hung on the wall in the living room.

One year Dan had a narrow escape with a bear and her three cubs. He came upon her as he walked near her den and she came at him, mouth open. But with his quickness, he was able to shoot her before she reached him. Dan was sure she would have just walked away when she saw him except for her cubs. Since the babies had lost their mother, Dan felt sad about it, but he had to shoot the cubs also. The bear skins were made into two rugs – one for in front of the fireplace in the living room and the three small skins in the other. They were a reminder of how close Dan came to death. My fears over his deer hunting became worse after this incident but it never stopped him from going the next year.

CHAPTER THIRTY ONE

"Citizenship"

"Dan, I need to get my United States Citizenship. What if the government here thinks because I'm German, I might be a part of this war?"

"Well, guess you should. Why don't you go to the court house in Oshkosh and see what it takes to become a citizen?"

I check the requirements and learn I need to take six classes of two hours each to learn about the history and government of the United States.

Gretchen wants to become a citizen too so we attend the classes together. I drive to Neenah, pick her up every Monday night and we go to the court house in Oshkosh.

The history of the United States is most interesting to me. Gretchen seems bored but picks up enough of the important points. We talk about what we have learned on our way home. Once in a while we go to a good movie after class.

Early September, 1941, we go to the court house to take the test. On the way we try to remember some of the important points.

"Who's our President," I ask.

"F. D. Roosevelt," Gretchen answers.

"How many colonies were there?"

"Thirteen."

"When was Independence Day?"

"July 4, 1776."

"Who'd the United States want to be free from?"

"England."

"I sure hope I can remember all the right stuff," I say. "Tests always made me nervous in school so I'm sure this one will be no different. How about you?"

"Oh," mumbles Gretchen, "I could take 'em or leave 'em. No big deal."

When we arrive and I reach for my exam paper, my hands are shaking but I calm down once I start reading the questions.

We both pass the exam and on September 22, 1941, we become proud citizens of the United States of America. I want Dan to come with me the day I become a citizen but he is too busy harvesting corn. Grandma Romberg takes care of the children for me.

Several weeks later, I receive a visitor. He's a gentleman in a black suit and says he's from the government. He asks me all kinds of questions about my life in Germany, who my parents were, do I have family there yet, why and when did I come to America. I feel so uneasy with all these questions – like he suspects me of something. Does he think I'm a spy hiding out on a farm in Wisconsin?

When he leaves, he seems satisfied but after that I'm sure when I run to the co-op in Larsen for Dan, I see a car following me. The car always stays far back but is still visible to me. The car never comes up our long driveway but goes on by when I turn in. This goes on for three or four months after I become a citizen and then I don't see it anymore. Guess he's learned I'm no threat to the United States of America.

Once again I think back on how often I'd questioned God in my prayers about being sent over here. Now that this war is on, it's so very clear to me that God had a better life planned for me and Gretchen than we'd have ever had back in Germany.

CHAPTER THIRTY TWO

"Accused of Stealing"

Hearing the door slam makes me jump. Dan storms into the kitchen with a look on his face I've never seen before. I send the boys out to play, check on Shirley in the bedroom and Carol in the bassinet. Then I wait for him to tell me what's wrong. I wait a couple minutes and then say, "What's wrong?"

When he doesn't answer right away, I walk over to him, put my arm around his waist and my head on his shoulder. Something terrible must have happened for him to act like this.

After several minutes he sighs and begins, "Went to the co-op today and had quite a shock, Heidi. Nobody would talk to me. Nobody. I'd say my usual greetings to the men I knew and they all turned their backs on me and left me standing there. After five or six of these I got to Charlie who didn't exactly turn his back but he, too, acted strange. Then he told me what's the matter."

"And what in the world could be wrong with everybody?"

"Well, it seems I've been stealing chickens at Ed's place."

"Stealing chickens! Who in the world would think such a terrible thing?"

"Apparently everybody," Dan says and with a gentle push away from me, he sits down at the table.

I sit down next to him and he tells me the story.

"Apparently Ed went out Tuesday night and found half his chickens gone and those left were flying around wild. He found a red handkerchief like I use in the chicken coop and he thinks because of the handkerchief, it was me."

"But you weren't anywhere near his place that night, Dan. You were at the Fireman's meeting at the Clayton Town Hall."

"I know. But when I told Charlie this, he shook his head and figures I could have been out there after the meeting. Said I'd left early a few times before and it all added up that I'd been doing this all along."

"This is ridiculous. Why in the world would you want to steal Ed's chickens?"

"Well, I sure wish I knew. Guess the only thing I can do is go see Ed and clear this thing up. I'll run over there after chores tonight."

Dan is gone for several hours and after putting the children to bed, I sit on the front steps waiting for him to come home. The night is warm with a near full moon and slight breeze from the north. Much as I'd like to enjoy its beauty all I can think of is who would accuse Dan of such a thing? My forehead creases into a frown as I run over our list of friends and neighbors and can't imagine who would do such a thing. Dan is always helping everybody, always been the kind of neighbor people admire. Obviously everybody likes him to vote him in as Fire Chief of Clayton Township.

He threshes their grain with his threshing machine, pulls people out of the mud with his heavy tractors and welds their broken machinery parts. I get weary trying to think of who it might be when Jacob Wilson comes to mind. Jacob didn't like how long it took Dan to get to his threshing this year. Wonder if he'd stoop so low as to spread such a story around?

While I'm mulling over how upset Jacob had been, Dan drives in the yard. I wait for him to come to the steps and watch his face as he sits down beside me.

"Well, what happened?" I ask.

"OK, ready for this? I couldn't convince Ed for one minute that I didn't take his chickens. He not only told me what a thief I was but proceeded to tell me how much everybody in the area hates my guts."

I gasp and put a hand to my mouth.

"I don't think he stopped ranting and raving about me for ten whole minutes and all the while he's doing it, I'm beginning to see something. People around here are jealous of me, Heidi. Of you and me and our farming success. When that thought hit me I could see right through this whole silly thing because Ed was actually happy to find a reason to tell me how he really feels."

"But why are they jealous? All you've ever been is good to everyone around by helping when needed. This is the thanks you get?"

"I don't know about everybody, but I can tell you Ed doesn't look at things that way. When I could finally get a word in I told him where I was that night and he just glared at me. Said he knew I'd been there but could have easily come to his place afterwards."

Dan pauses and wipes his brow. Then looking down at the ground continues, "After listening to Ed's story, I was about to defend myself some more when his hired hand, Luke, came into the barn. He stood at the door looking at the ground as he shuffled his feet back and forth and finally said to Ed, 'Found the chickens. They're out in the back woods, roosting in the lower branches and that, that handkerchief you found, is mine. I dropped it last time I fed the chickens.'"

Dan looks at me, sadness in his eyes and says, "It seems the hired hand heard Ed ranting at me and had the decency to come in and confess that he let the chickens out by mistake. At the time he was too scared to say so. He let this story get out about me because it took him off the hook but he started to feel guilty about it and so came forward."

I reach over and take Dan's hand and he continues, "Ed, of course, didn't know what to make of it all and so just stood there for some time before he finally told Luke he should get going after the chickens. Then he turned to me and apologized. But you know what, Heidi, he'd said so many ugly things to me that I never said a word. Just turned and left."

We sit on the steps for a long time after Dan's story and wonder just how widespread the things Ed had said are. How many others are jealous of our success? How many other neighbors really hate us?

After this incident, Dan never trusts his friends and neighbors again. He still helps when asked, still as good to them as he'd ever been, but he holds his friendship back and is no more the outgoing, friendly man he'd always been.

CHAPTER THIRTY THREE

"Bad Habits"

Although it isn't easy for me to admit it, I don't really have a lot of patience. Oh, I do with the children most of the time and try to with Dan but not when it comes to my work. If everything doesn't go my way, I get upset. Over the years I've learned some swear words from the hired men. Dan rarely swears but I find it an outlet for my anger and do it often – too often.

Sometimes I say things in German like "Ach mein Gott in Himmel." (Oh my God in heaven.) But I soon learn the English "son-of-a-bitch" and "bastard" and use them regularly.

Hard as I try not to swear in front of the children, I realize I have a problem when two-year-old Carol lets loose with my swear words. If I scold her, she defies me and keeps right on. When I scold the older children about swearing, they quickly stop and hang their head in shame but not Carol. I figure she's too young to understand what I mean. Scolding only seems to urge her on to do more.

When Carol swears around home, it isn't that much of a problem. When she does it out shopping for groceries though, I become concerned. I never know when she'll burst forth with "You son of a bitch," or "Stop that, you bastard."

Of course, this language is most intolerable in church. Every Sunday I try my hardest to keep her happy during the service so she won't get frustrated and let loose with some of her choice words. I let her walk around on the floor in front of our pew, play with a handkerchief by wrapping my hand in it like a bandage or give her my bracelets to play with. If she ever does slip and say something, I explain she must have heard it from the hired man. This special treatment for Carol bothers Shirley. She is expected to sit still with her hands folded in her lap.

One Sunday on the way home from church Shirley asks, "How come Carol gets to play in church and I don't?" I stutter around a moment and then tell her the truth. "Well, Shirley, I don't have to worry about your language in church but I can't trust Carol. She's too little to know some of her language is unacceptable there. Well, really anywhere." Then I gave her a hug and think, *"I have to get more control over my mouth. I just must. Oh, God, please help me overcome my bad swearing habit."*

CHAPTER THIRTY FOUR

"Dan's Injury"

"Momma, Momma," Harvey yells as he races up to me while I'm hanging clothes on the line. I drop the sheet I am pinning up and say, "What's wrong?"

"Daddy – Daddy – hurt himself. Bad."

"Where? How?"

"Come on, come on. He's in the shed."

I race to the machine shed behind Harvey and find Dan stooped over the workbench holding his left hand. Blood is oozing from his fingers.

Running over to him I ask "What happened?" I push a wooden box up to him and say, "Here. Sit down."

He sits and good thing because he looks as white as the sheet I was trying to hang on the line. I think he'd have fainted if he wouldn't have sat when he did.

He slowly removes his right hand and I see his middle finger is badly cut. In fact, the end has been smashed.

"Run. Get me a towel," I say to Harvey.

"I - - I - - was set – setting the jack to work on the trailer tire when it sli – slipped and caught my finger," Dan mumbles.

Harvey comes with a towel and I carefully wrap Dan's hand.

"We need to get to the doctor. Now!" I say. Dan nods and slowly rises from the box.

* * * * *

Dan lost the tip of his middle finger but the doctor said it would heal and he'd be fine. Poor man walked the floor all night that first night and when the wound healed, his finger nail grows and curves around the end of that finger. We thank God he wasn't hurt worse because he could have lost his whole finger – maybe his hand. Made me realize just how dangerous farm work can be with all the moving parts of the machinery. This lesson made us more conscious about being careful.

CHAPTER THIRTY FIVE

"Family Reunion"

Yesterday was the Thiel Reunion in Hatten Park, New London. It's held every year, the second Sunday of July. Dan really loves getting together with relatives and I try hard to enjoy them too. But it isn't easy when every year somebody says something like, "Oh, Heidi, I see you're still just as heavy as ever." This year it was Kimball. Last year it was Loren. Every year it's somebody who has to loudly exclaim something about how heavy I am.

I remember the Romberg Reunion last fall when Dr. Fred Romberg stuck up for me. "Everybody can't be a size sixteen. At least her weight is distributed nicely and not sitting in one spot like mine," he said shaking his stomach up and down with both hands. Sure made me feel good to have somebody stick up for me once.

I've tried to lose weight many times. None of the diets in the magazines have helped. Seems I last maybe a week or so and then can't stand it. Dan complains that I'm crabby when I go on these things and has told me many times to quit worrying about my weight. He likes me the way I am. But I still worry anyway. He doesn't get the remarks about weight that I do.

In fact, Dan is really too thin. If only I could give him some of my pounds. He eats all he wants and works it off out in the barn and the field.

I've tried water pills and they take the weight off real nice for a few days. But that's all it is too – water. Not fat.

Oh, why do I have such a time with this? Guess it has to be the years I first got to America and never had enough to eat - some psychological thing haunting me from the past. How I'd lie in bed nights, stomach growling and aching, and could do nothing about it. Well, now I do have food around. Whenever I want something, it's there.

Enough feeling sorry for myself. Time to get at the baking here today. Boys will be home from school soon and will want something to eat. Guess I'll bake chocolate chip cookies for them – and me!

CHAPTER THIRTY SIX

"My Garden"

Every spring I ask Dan to plow my garden area for me. It's at the end of one of our fields and easy for him to do. I plant carrots, radishes, onions, beans, cucumbers and beets. It's a lot of work planting it as well as keeping the weeds down all summer long. Sometimes I wonder though whether it's worth all the trouble.

The boys are old enough now at ages nine and twelve to help with this work. Leslie helps the most because Harvey also helps Dan in the fields.

Harvey is old enough to drive our big tractor too. It's such a slow-moving thing I don't worry about him doing so at all. He actually started driving it at age ten and back then I worried a lot about him.

10-Year-old Harvey driving our first tractor

Harvey was also good with our big draft horses. I also drove them and got along much better with them than the tractor. One team we called Tom and Jerry. They were like pets to us. They were well-trained and no problem at all. Harvey was good at harnessing those horses too and he knew how to care for them. Actually, both boys knew what to do and were such a help to us.

But as soon as the tractor hit the farm, I knew the days of driving horses were numbered. It was going to be easier to take care of a tractor than horses.

One frustrating thing about my garden though is every year when the men cultivate the field near it, they wind up driving over parts of it – ruining the vegetables. Seems no amount of scolding stops them. All they do is whine something like, "Well, it's hard making the turn right there. Sorry if it causes you some trouble."

"Well, try a little harder next time, will you?" I plead.

But I know from past experience it'll happen again. Maybe a fence would help. Guess I'll have to work on that idea. Either that or forget the whole thing.

CHAPTER THIRTY SEVEN

"Aunt Greta"

One gloomy, rainy afternoon the phone rings and it's Anne. Aunt Greta is in the hospital with what they think is a stroke. When Dan finishes the chores so he can watch the children, I drive into Neenah to the hospital.

When I walk into the room, my heart sinks as I see Aunt Greta's frail body lying in bed, tubes run from a machine to her nose and she barely breathes. Anne sits by the bed holding her hand, tears streaking down her face. She is slumped in the chair by the bed, her cheeks pale and her gray hair drawn tightly back in a bun. She smiles at me and says, "Oh, Heidi, thanks for coming." I shake her hand and ask, "What happened?"

"Well," Anne says, "I stopped over to see Ma and Pa and Ma was rocking in her chair but mumbling strangely. When I tried to talk to her I couldn't understand a thing she said. Then Pa told me she'd been limping before she sat and her right arm was hanging strangely by her side."

"When was this?" I asked.

"Last night. So I told him something was very wrong and she had to see a doctor right away. I called Dr. Orbison and he said to bring her straight to the hospital. Pa had to carry her to the car and into the hospital. She couldn't walk at all by then."

"Oh, my, Anne," I mumble.

"Well, Doctor says it's a stroke and since her right side is paralyzed, a bad one."

Aunt Greta is in the hospital a week with no improvement. Anne decides to take her to her house and care for her. At 68, and with the farm chores to do, Pa isn't able to handle her.

I stop at Anne's to see Aunt Greta as often as I can – usually when I take the eggs in to sell at the Krambo Store and buy groceries. She always seems glad to see me and starts to cry. She can only mumble, always in German, but now and then I do understand a few words.

As I sit next to her, listening to her soft chatter, I can't help but remember how cruel she was to me the three years Gretchen and I lived with her and Uncle Alfred. In all the visits Dan and I made to see them over the years, she never once brought up the past.

My seeing her now is not based on gratitude or real love for her. And yet, I can't help but pity her.

Each time I visit I hold her hand and say a prayer that God would give her courage and strength. She seems to like this because she smiles her crooked little smile (since one side of her face is paralyzed) and nods her head.

Often I pray for Anne because what she is doing has to be difficult. But Anne refuses to put her Ma in any home – insists it's no trouble to care for her. Bless that Anne!

Uncle Alfred, meanwhile, continues to live alone on the old home farm. Sometimes I stop in to see him after visiting Aunt Greta and take him a homemade apple pie or some cookies. He seems to appreciate this and I have no quarrel with him. Somehow the past never comes up with Uncle Alfred either. Probably just as well. He wasn't the problem anyway. Aunt Greta was the mean one and as often as I'd like to tell her how awful she was, I can't do it. I just can't. I figure she's suffering enough lying in that hospital bed.

Uncle Alfred dies three years after Aunt Greta's stroke. Aunt Greta dies ten years after Uncle Alfred.

CHAPTER THIRTY EIGHT

"Gretchen Divorces"

"Hello," I answer the phone out of breath from running up the basement steps.

"Heidi?" Gretchen answers.

"Yes, it's me."

"Have made up my mind. Sam and I are through. Had it out last night. He's calling the lawyer today and we're getting started on the divorce."

"Oh, Gretchen, I'm so sorry you couldn't work things out. He's determined to take up with Vivian then, huh?"

After a short hesitation, Gretchen says, "Ye – yes – I guess so although he wouldn't come right out and say it. I know he was over there last night before he came home. I was sitting in the living room and saw him come out their back door. Then he walked around to our front door and came in as if I wouldn't notice what he was doing. Sickening!"

"Well, I'm sure you've done everything possible to stay married but it takes both of you. You can't do it alone. Is there anything I can do to help? Watch the kids for you?"

"No. They're all in school now and he's going to schedule our appointment when school's on so no, but thanks anyway."

I hang up the phone and sink into my rocker by the stove.

Poor Gretchen. Moreso, poor Pam, Kate and Scott. Gretchen understands all this. They don't. They're only five, seven and eight. Too young to really understand. And oh dear, this brings back memories when I lost my father at the age of seven. My oh my how my life did change after he was gone. Poor kids. No father around.

I sit and remember many of the awful feelings I had after Papa died. Of course my pain was moreso because Mama was so mean to me. She always had been but was worse after Papa died. At least Gretchen's children will have her. She treats them with love – something I never had from my mother.

As I finish my wash and hang things on the line, I can't stop thinking about Gretchen and Sam's children. Making bread later on I pound and knead and poke out my frustration and sadness on the dough. Somehow it helps relieve some of the tension.

"I'll just have to stop in often and offer my help to all of them – not just Gretchen," I mutter to myself.

I've made this vow before and meant it and I'm making it again. Because I know how awful it is to be without a father, I will stay married to Dan no matter what goes on. My children will always have their father around.

CHAPTER THIRTY NINE

"Hired Hands"

At ages fifteen and twelve, Harvey and Leslie are now old enough to do the work of any hired hands. They know some day this place will belong to them. This should make them far more attentive to everything as they learn how to be good farmers. Hopefully they will care more about being sure the gates are shut so the cows don't get into the corn and the pigs into the potatoes. Such a time we've had when the hired hands weren't so careful. One of the worst things on a farm is to hear someone shout, "The cows are in the corn!" Means drop everything, chase them all down and get them back to the barnyard. It takes hours sometimes.

Now that we don't need hired hands anymore, I can't help but remember how strange some of these fellows were. Mark, our first hired hand, lived with us just after we were married. He was our best and I still miss him at times. Our other hired hands lived nearby and only came for the day.

There was Jesse, a middle-aged man in his late thirties – the nephew of a neighbor. He had few teeth and what he had were black. He'd tease the boys sometimes until they cried and Dan or I'd have to step in and stop him.

Little Fritz was at least in his sixties and no more than five feet tall. He lived above the garage at the Wilson's and helped more than one farmer. He'd help them with their chores each morning and night and us in the fields during the day. He was handy with small repairs and good with machinery.

Harry and Emma came to us right after they were married and were also some of our best. They lived upstairs but ate their meals with us. Emma helped me with the house work, Harry in the barn and fields. When Emma's grandfather died, he gave her a small inheritance and they left us. They bought a fifty-acre farm near Wild Rose. We visited back and forth a while but then life got too busy for us and we sort of lost touch. I still miss her. I always knew when she was happy because she'd whistle happy tunes as she worked. And she'd scowl when she was sad.

The Farm

CHAPTER FORTY

"The Storm"

Late one hot, humid July afternoon I go out to the chicken coop to gather eggs. There is a strange stillness to the day with a yellowish haze in the sky. On my way back to the house, I look to the north and see huge black clouds forming and the wind begins to pick up. I quickly take my pail of eggs around to the cellar door. By the time I get there, the wind is much stronger. I yell, "Shirley, Carol, where are you?"

I faintly hear Shirley say, "Upstairs."

"Quick, come down to the cellar at once. There's a storm coming."

I run to the kitchen window and look out. In the short time since I got in the house, the trees are whipping back and forth, bending to the point of breaking and the sky is black.

"Is Leslie still out in the field?" I yell.

The girls hurry into the room and Shirley says, "Gee, I think so. I heard Daddy tell him to go to the north forty and cultivate the corn."

"Quick, you two get down in the basement and don't come up until I call you. I'm going to get Leslie with the car because that tractor's too slow to get him home here fast enough."

I run out to the car and start it up, back away from the garage and turn down the lane to the north forty. By now rain is falling. I look ahead and see the tractor coming about half a mile away. Before I reach him, pea-size hail bounces on the windshield and hood of the car. I drive faster over the rough lane up to the tractor and yell out the window, "Hurry! Get in. Leave the tractor. It'll be alright."

Leslie quickly gets in the car and says, "Am I glad to see you, Mom." He rubs his arms and says, "Gee that hail hurts when it hits."

I back into the field to turn around. Just as I make the turn back to the house, a tree branch flies across the windshield. I hit the brakes and close my eyes. When I open them, the wind has blown the branch off the car hood and I continue on. I make my way through blinding rain and hail to the front steps and park the car. We both get out and struggle against the wind to the steps. The wind is blowing so hard neither one of us can reach them.

Motioning toward the side of the house, I yell, "Let's go round to the cellar door. It's more protected there." We make our way around the side of the house and because it is easier, safely get in the cellar door.

"Shirley, Carol, are you OK?" I yell when I shut the door.

"We're fine," said Shirley. "Did you get Leslie home OK?"

"Yes, he's here," I answer as Leslie and I run down the cellar steps by the girls. "We have to stay here until that awful wind stops. I just hope Dad and Harvey are OK over at the neighbors."

We stay in the basement for an hour before the howling winds cease and the hail stops. Now only heavy rain is falling. When we get upstairs, we look out to see tree branches down everywhere. Part of the machine shed roof is hanging off the side of the building. I look to the sky and see the black clouds are moving to the southeast.

Turning to the east window, I look out at the grain field and see it nearly flattened to the ground. I gasp and say, "Oh, dear. How will we ever be able to harvest that field now."

Later that evening when Dan and Harvey get home, they tell how they were safe at the Anderson's farm which is farther north. On their way home, they discovered a tornado had gone through and taken the Schultz's barn down. They stopped to see if they needed any help and found no animals or people were hurt. When they found everyone was alright, they came on home.

When Dan sees the flattened grain field he says, "Looks worse than it really is. Most of it will stand again. This happened a couple times at the home place and once the rain ended, the grain straightened up enough so it could be harvested. It'll be OK."

The next day we all go over to help the Schultz's. I make bread that morning and take a couple loaves along as well as a dish of scalloped potatoes and ham. It's devastating to see the damage done by that awful storm – whatever was once their barn is nothing but a heap of broken boards. Trees are down and debris is scattered everywhere. While the men begin work on the cleanup, several of us women start a noon meal for everyone. In and around preparing the meal, we help with the cleanup.

On our way home late that afternoon, we can't help but feel thankful that we had such little damage in comparison to the mess we'd worked on all day. Although it was going to be a long time before we had our own place back to normal, the Schultz's would have it much harder.

CHAPTER FORTY ONE

"Hay Fever"

Every August, when the ragweed blossoms, I develop hay fever. My nose runs continually, my eyes itch and burn and at times I feel short of breath. Although it's difficult to do, I keep right on with most of my daily work, sniffing and blowing my nose but when the problems get real bad, I must lay down and rest a while.

August is also fair time – the time of year when the children get involved with projects for the fair. All summer they attend 4-H meetings and classes to prepare their projects. The boys work on raising a calf to a young heifer. They also raise a pig. When not working on the farm, they are busy with these two projects. The animals are shown in different classes at the fair – some for how well the animals have developed, some for showmanship.

The girls are in sewing and baking. For sewing, Shirley is making a skirt and Carol a scarf. For baking, Shirley is developing her special chocolate cake and Carol chocolate chip cookies. Their practicing makes for good things to eat and they both do well in the kitchen. When they need help with their projects, I am there for them and it's fun watching them learn.

The day all projects have to be at the fair is a busy one. Dan helps the boys with the animals and I help the girls get their things registered.

Because of my hay fever, it isn't easy for me to be out in public. People stare at me and my red eyes and nose making me wish I was home. Dr. Orbison gave me a u-shaped device which helps me. It fits in my nose and has small medicated sponges on each side. It helps keep my nose from continuous running. When people stare at me because of this shiny metal thing in my nose, I feel so conspicuous. Because of this, I don't attend much of the fair. When I do get to some of the events, I find myself cowering in the back of the crowd so I'm not noticed.

Harvey and Leslie both win blue ribbons for their heifers and pigs. Harvey gets a blue ribbon for showmanship for his heifer and red for his pig. Leslie gets a red for showmanship of his heifer and white for his pig. Leslie needs to practice showing his animals a bit more next year.

Shirley gets a blue ribbon for her skirt and so does Carol for her scarf. They both get red ribbons on their baking. Although they would have liked blue ribbons for everything, what they do get is still an accomplishment.

This season of the year is so miserable for me that I often feel depressed. Try as I might, I want summer to end so this misery is over. The fall freeze finally does come early October and the ragweed is gone. My symptoms disappear and I'm finally back to normal. How wonderful!

CHAPTER FORTY TWO

"Mother's Day"

It's seven p.m. on Mother's Day. I lay on the bed in my spare bedroom upstairs very upset. My eyes hurt from crying all afternoon. What started as such a happy day turned into one of the ugliest, and all over a bitter argument with Dan. It was silly. Stupid, really.

The day began so nice. Dan came in from the morning chores, walked up behind me at the kitchen stove and told me to close my eyes. I heard him close the dining room door and call all four children. A few minutes later he called me from a crack in the door and when I got there, covered my eyes with his hands and said, "Walk."

I walked a couple steps and he took his hands away. There on the dining room table stood a gorgeous purple mum plant surrounded by several wrapped packages. The plant was huge with at least a dozen large flowers on it. They all said, "Happy Mother's Day" at once.

What a thrill to have such special treatment on such a special day.

After breakfast, I ask, "Why can't we go over to your Ma's after supper tonight instead of all afternoon."

Dan sounded defensive, "Why so late? We always go over there in the afternoon on Mother's Day. Why not this year?"

"Well," I said. "It'd be nice to stay here once."

His voice rose with, "Oh, I see. You really don't want to spend time at Ma's. You know I'm tired of your attitude about her. I think you'd rather not have anything to do with her, ever. Take Sunday mornings for instance, when she calls for a ride to church."

I interrupt with, "Now, wait a minute. You've said yourself she should be riding with her daughter, who happens to live right across the road from her."

"I never said that. Can't you get anything straight? How dumb are you?"

And we were off and running. The argument turned ugly when he started calling me names, something he usually winds up doing. Seems when he can't come up with anything worthwhile to say, he starts that and I'm sick of it. So I shouted back. The girls covered their ears, obviously upset, but when we get into one of those we're in some sort of oblivion and can't stop.

We never did get to church. I went upstairs and locked myself in the spare bedroom and left them to themselves for lunch. Soon afterwards they left for Ma's. It certainly was apparent he thought more of her than me.

Mid-afternoon I went downstairs and made sandwiches, putting them in the refrigerator. I wrote a note to the girls about what they should do for supper. Then I took my movie magazines, climbed the stairs back to the spare bedroom and locked myself in. I intended to stay here until tomorrow morning.

Once I lay back down I start thinking again and the tears come. I cry myself to sleep and wake up around 4:30 when I hear the car drive in. Harvey calls my name when he walks into the kitchen but I don't answer. I hear footsteps on the stairs, then a rap on the door. "Mom, Mom," Harvey calls. I hear Leslie and the girls whispering behind him.

"I'm here, resting," I tell them. "Go have some supper and leave me alone."

So, what do I do next? Dan will give me the cold shoulder treatment I'm giving him until one of us finally gives in and we make up – probably days from now.

Some "Happy Mother's Day."

Mother's Day

CHAPTER FORTY THREE

"A Misunderstanding"

I pick up the phone and cheerfully say, "Hello."

"It's Anne. If you don't keep your mouth shut, I'm going to shut it for you!"

The bang of her receiver rings in my ear and I slam my phone down in its cradle.

"The nerve of that woman. Who does she think she is talking to me like that? And whatever have I said that has her so angry?"

That evening Anne and her husband George drive in the yard and it isn't long before I find out why she's so upset. They stay for over an hour while she rants and raves at me about my telling the entire Ladies Aid at church about a problem they have on the farm. One day last week she confided in me about some troubles she and George were having. I would never tell anyone anything like that and she knows it.

I say, "I never told Ruth anything about you and furthermore – "

"Oh, yes you did. I saw you and her in the kitchen at church laughing and carrying on after the church Mission Festival. It sure looked like you were talking about me."

"Ruth? In the church kitchen?" I ask, my mind racing to remember what it was I'd talked to Ruth about. It certainly wasn't the subject Anne thinks it was. I'd never talk about her like that.

"No, no, Anne," I blurt. "We were not laughing about you. I never said a word about your problem. Not a word. I'd never do that."

"Well, we'll just see about that because I'm not one bit satisfied with your weak denial. I know what I saw and it was just too close to our talk the day before for you to be telling the truth. You're lying!"

We sit glaring at each other for several minutes. Didn't seem to make much sense to keep denying I'd done what she thought so I'll just sit here and wait.

Finally Anne gets up and stomps toward the door. Opening it, she says, "This isn't settled by any means. Come on George." They leave, slamming the door behind them.

I sit on the couch in shock. I've seen Anne upset before but never this angry. Whatever am I going to do?

It's Sunday and on my way out of church, Anne grabs me by the arm and starts rattling away at me about my talk with Ruth again. I pull my arm back and walk away. I go down the side aisle and cover my face with my hymnal so nobody will see that I'm crying. I just can't help it. This has me so upset. I go to the pastor's office and knock on the door.

"Yes," Pastor Gilson asks.

"I - - I need to talk to you, Pastor, if I may."

He tells me to come in and I explain that my sister-in-law is accusing me of something I never did and she refuses to believe me. Pastor and I visit a while and he thinks perhaps a meeting between the three of us might help clear the matter up. He offers to call her and set up a convenient time.

Drying my eyes, I apologize for taking up his time and thank him.

Pastor calls me that afternoon and tells me the meeting will be at 4:00 at my house.

When I tell Dan about the meeting he says, "I'm taking the boys fishing this afternoon so I won't be here. You'll have to get out of this mess you've made yourself."

"Well, I'm sure glad to know where you stand in this. It certainly isn't by my side, is it?"

Dan shakes his head and leaves. My immediate thought is, "What's that verse in my favorite hymn 'What a Friend We Have in Jesus?' Goes something like this – Do thy friends despise, forsake thee, Take it to the Lord in prayer. In his arms he'll take and shield thee, thou wilt find a solace there. – Looks like my only real friend here is going to be Jesus. Well, maybe Pastor too."

When we all sit down at 4·00 p m , Pastor begins our meeting with a prayer asking God's help to solve this disagreement and for all to forgive one another.

When Pastor finishes, Anne begins to rant at me about telling Ruth and the entire Ladies Aid a problem she'd discussed with me. When she takes a breath I again deny I said anything about her problem to Ruth or anyone else.

Pastor says, "Anne, Heidi has denied she did what you say, why don't you believe her?"

"Because I know what she's like. She'll do anything for a laugh and she and Ruth were carrying on and on after the Mission Festival."

Pastor looks at me. I stare back thinking this is doing no good.

Pastor then says, "But appearances can be deceiving, Anne. Did you hear anything said?"

"No. I didn't have to."

"Heidi," Pastor turns toward me, "You still say you weren't discussing Anne's problem with Ruth?"

"That's right. I never did. I don't remember exactly what Ruth and I talked about but it was definitely not what Anne thinks it was. I'd never do that."

Anne snorts and folds her arms in what appears to be disgust.

We all sit in silence for a couple minutes that seem like an eternity. Finally, Anne says, "This isn't doing a bit of good. I'm through sitting here listening to her lies. And just so you know, George and I are leaving St. Paul's. We're going to the Community Center where they act like Christians."

She and George get up and although Pastor tries to urge them to wait and work this out, they brush past him to the door.

After Anne and George leave, Pastor says, "Heidi, this situation is more complicated than a simple misunderstanding. As I see things, she is a very stubborn woman and harbors a great deal of jealousy toward you."

Then he turns toward me, lays his hand on my arm, looks me in the eye and says, "Now, it's just you and me. Do you want to change anything at all about your side of the story?"

I look straight back at him and say, "No. What I said was the truth."

"All right you've done your part in trying to solve this thing and make peace. Now it's up to her. I hope she didn't mean it that they're leaving the church over this but if she comes to me, I'll be talking to her again about letting this go."

After Pastor leaves I sit on my couch in the living room for a long time thinking and praying over this misunderstanding. Then I remember what the Fortune Teller told me so many years ago – that a dark-haired woman would give me much trouble. Anne has dark hair. I wonder if that prediction is coming true? I sigh and mutter to myself, "Only time will tell whether Anne ever gets over this mistaken idea."

CHAPTER FORTY FOUR

"Up North"

This summer we had the best crop of clover seed ever. When the check arrives, Dan says, "This extra money needs to be invested in something. It's well known that land is one of the best investments there is. When the money is tied up in land, it's not as handy to fritter away like if it's in a savings account. Remember what I found out last fall on my way home from deer hunting? This realtor in Pembine told me about 80 acres of land near there with a lake on it."

"Oh, yes," I answer. "It sounded like just what we've been thinking about."

"It will be neat to have our own place up north to visit and it will also be great for deer hunting. I won't have so far to go every year."

The next Saturday we pile the kids in the car and drive the one hundred fifty miles north to Pembine. I have a picnic lunch for us and we are excited for the adventure ahead. It will be fun exploring this property to see if it meets our expectations.

We stop at the realtor's office and get a map with directions. The place is located about ten miles south of Pembine and when we turn off on the gravel road, three deer scamper across in front of us. The girls squeal with delight and Leslie says, "Hey, Dad, too bad we don't have the shotgun along."

"Right," says Dan, "But have to be careful we don't shoot any until the hunting season or we'll be in big trouble."

"Oh, yeah," says Leslie. "I forgot."

"Good to know they're around here though, huh?" Dan remarks with a grin.

After snaking up and down hills for several miles, we come to a corner of the property. We park the car and with Dan leading the way, begin our walk with Harvey, Leslie, Shirley, Carol and me following. It's slow going with tall grass and lots of brush to work our way through.

"Look at all the different kinds of trees there are," says Dan. "Maple, oak, white birch, quaking aspen and pine. I'll bet we'll be seeing all kinds of small animals too. Rabbits, squirrels and I'll bet the rarely seen Side-hill Gouger."

"Side-hill Gouger," repeats Leslie." What's that?"

"Oh, it's a strange little critter designed to go around a hill. One front leg and one back leg are shorter than the other side. Makes it easy to walk around hills – the shorter side for the upper part and the longer side for the other."

"Oh Dad, you're kidding, right?" asks Leslie.

The girls chime in with similar comments but Dan laughs and points ahead to a bush, "Hey, I think I just saw one! Better keep your eyes peeled."

We struggle along for about an hour and then come to the top of a hill. We look down and spot a small lake sparkling in the sunshine. Dan studies the map and says, "This property is on three sides of that lake down there. The farthest side, to the west, belongs to a Baptist Summer Camp. Looks like about three-quarters of the lake would be ours." Pointing to the map he continues. "There's a spring that runs into the lake here, and out over here. It's a fresh-water lake which is nice."

We continue walking toward the lake and the children have to see how cold the water is. They bend down and splash around in the water. They find it warm and wish they could go swimming but not today.

We discover a clearing and spread a blanket out for our picnic lunch, positioning ourselves so we can enjoy the lake while we eat. I find myself falling in love with the place and a glance at Dan tells me he, too, likes it very much.

Leslie, still bothered by Dan's story of the Side-hill Gouger, looks at his Dad and says, "I don't believe that stuff about short legs on one side, Dad."

Dan just grins and takes a bite of his chicken sandwich while the children excitedly discuss the critter amongst themselves.

We buy the property and begin plans to build a cabin on it. Dan has had experience building and with the help of the boys and Gretchen's new husband, Jim, it won't take long. Dan plans to begin with a cement slab for the foundation with a huge fireplace in the center. It will be built so that the fireplace heats the entire cabin. There will be a living room with a small kitchen on one side and two bedrooms off the other.

The next summer with the help of our brother-in-law, Jim, Dan and the boys make several trips up to Pembine to build the cabin. They camp out in a tent until they get the foundation built. Then Dan constructs the fireplace. Next, they tackle the four walls. By fall, the cabin is roughed in, with walls up and roof on.

One three-day weekend Dan and I go up to build the steps from the place we park the car up to the cabin. What a lot of work it is hauling water, pail after pail, but by the end of the weekend, we have our steps. Now work can be done on the inside during the fall and winter. It's going to be a beautiful place.

Dan, Carol and me up North

Dan and me up North

CHAPTER FORTY FIVE

"Christmas Melancholy"

Christmas is such a wonderful time of year. I enjoy the weeks of preparation before it, the extra church services with all the special music and the shopping for gifts. I bake fruit cake, nut bread, cookies and candy and hide a lot of it so we'll have it for the busy holiday season. While I work, I'm humming Christmas carols like "O Tannenbaum," "Silent Night" and "Joy to the World."

Shopping for the children is such fun because Dan and I try hard to get them at least one special gift they really want. The girls almost always want some sort of doll. This year they'll each get a bride doll. I saw some beautiful ones at Sears last week. The boys want new rifles and Dan will be checking into them. Dan is easy because he always needs clothes. Of course, the children get some too.

We open our gifts Christmas morning before chores. Dan and I never have to worry about when to get up that morning because the girls come in and shake us around 4:30 – 5:00 a.m. telling us "It's Christmas morning. Santa came. Get up, get up!" So we crawl out of bed, into our slippers and robes and shuffle out to the living room where our huge Christmas tree towers over us. White popcorn strings weave back and forth from top to bottom and the ornaments glimmer from the lights. I always love the wonderful pine scent that fills the living room and spills over into the entire downstairs.

What fun it is watching the excited faces of our children as they strip the paper from each present. Their happy shouts of "oh, boy – I love it – thanks Santa" fill the room and my heart. It's a wonderful time.

When the hustle and bustle is over, I sink into a deep melancholy. I think back on my life in Germany and the happy years before Papa died. How awful it was to get the news that he had died and how cruel Mama always was. Then I'm at the last Christmas Eve church service with my best friend, Emma. I remember that service as if it were yesterday. Then I'm in America and remember how nasty Aunt Greta was. By now I'm overwhelmed with sadness and have to get away for a while. So each year, after Christmas Day, I go to Neenah and stay with Gretchen and her family. She and her new husband, Jim, have two little girls, Sherrie and Cindy, besides her Pam, Kate and Scott. It's crowded in their little house but everyone seems to enjoy my presence.

Being away from Dan and the children seems to jar me out of my melancholy. I realize how much they mean to me and how good my life really is here in America, much better than it ever would have been in Germany. When Dan comes to get me, I hug him hard and long. On the way home he tells me how he and the children missed me and he hopes I'm OK again. I smile at him and say, "Oh, yes. I'm OK again."

Dan and me on our way to church

CHAPTER FORTY SIX

"Rusty"

"Momma, Momma, come quick. Rusty's sick," cries Carol one hot July afternoon.

"He won't get up. Just lays and pants. Come quick."

I hurry behind Carol down the hill to the barn where Rusty lays in the shade of the milk house, near the water tank.

Rusty, our watchdog – part collie, part Irish setter, part husky – is on his side, tongue hanging out, panting heavily. He's soaking wet and full of mud. I stoop down beside him and touch his nose. It's cool like it should be. I say, "What's going on old boy? Have you been down by the creek again? Too hot for you today?"

Then I notice bits of grey fur on one side of his mouth and know pretty much what's wrong with him.

Rusty

"Quick," I say, "Get that pail and bring me some water from the tank. Then run and get me a towel from the bathroom."

Carol grabs the pail, dips it into the tank and brings it to me. I take handfuls and give Rusty some to drink. He laps frantically at my hand. I give him more. Then I gently sprinkle water over his dirty body and rub as much mud off him as I can. Slowly his breathing returns to normal and he rolls his big brown eyes up at me as if to say, "Thanks."

Rusty loves chasing rabbits and that's what he'd just been doing. He must have caught at least part of one by the looks of the hair in his teeth, and he overdid on a hot and humid summer day.

"He's OK, Carol. Just wore himself out chasing a rabbit. See the hair in his teeth there? Looks like the rabbit got away but poor Rusty is done in from the chase and playing in the muddy creek."

I give Carol a quick hug and say, "Good thing you came to get me Sweetheart, because he's dehydrated and needed water bad. But he's going to be fine. He's just tuckered out. You stay by him and watch. If he acts worse again, come get me."

On my way back to the house, my thoughts turn to what a wonderful pet Rusty has been. We got him from the Andersons as a six-month-old puppy and he has been the best dog we ever had. Over the years we'd had several but Rusty outshone them all.

Living a mile from anyone can be scary at times when strangers drive in the yard – especially salesmen. Rusty always hears them come and loudly barks their arrival. Unless I call him off, they never get out of their cars.

I smile to myself over the time Rusty was in the house when a salesman knocked on our door. I opened the kitchen door to the sun porch and when Rusty leaped on the outer door and looked out the window at him barking wildly, did he ever run back to his car. Oh, he's wonderful for protection.

He's so good with the kids too. The girls harness him up to their wagon and he pulls them around the yard.

When the boys go hunting, he's great at retrieving the pheasants or ducks they shoot.

And he loves to ride in the truck anywhere – down to the field or to the co-op for supplies. He sits in the cab straight as any human and puffs himself up so he can see out the window. When Dan gets home and tries to get him out of the cab, Rusty protests with a soft, low growl. Dan always figures it means he isn't ready to stop "playing human" yet so he leaves the door open for when he is ready to come out. Sooner or later Rusty jumps down and runs off.

I go back to my ironing and when I finish about half an hour later, decide to check on Rusty. Eight-year-old Carol is lying beside him, her head on his stomach, sleeping. Rusty is lying with his head up, eyes bright and alert again, tongue hanging to one side of his mouth. He looks at Carol, then at me as if to say, "Aw Ma, let her stay. She's my buddy."

CHAPTER FORTY SEVEN

"Fire"

September 19, 1950, starts out like any other busy fall day. The men are finishing up with our third crop of hay this year and I'm canning beans. I just took a batch from the boiler on the stove and am lining the jars up on the cupboard to cool when Harvey bursts in the door shouting, "Fire! Fire in the barn!"

"Mein Gott in Himmel!" I say. "Get Dad. Look! He's coming out of the machine shop."

Harvey runs up to Dan telling what he'd found and Dan yells to me, "Call the fire department. Hurry!"

I ring up the operator and say, "Heidi Romberg here. Please send the fire department. Our barn is on fire!"

I run out the door, down the hill and into the barn. Smoke fills the far end and flames shoot out from the ceiling of the bull pen. The bull is snorting and pawing the floor.

"Quick," Dan yells, "Get the bull out in the barnyard."

I hurry to open the pen door and Harvey waves at the bull so he runs out the door to the barnyard.

Dan hurries back to the house and brings several of our glass fire retardant bulbs. He runs to the ramp that leads to the barn's second floor with me tight behind. Smoke fills the entire hay loft. Dan climbs into the loft and breaks the bulbs against the ceiling beams. The liquid sprays over the haymow.

My heart is in my mouth as I watch Dan climb around the beams. Then I hear a wonderful sound – the siren of the fire trucks. First comes the Chief and then two tank trucks. Several other trucks and cars with volunteer firemen follow. Soon water is being sprayed into the haymow. More trucks and cars stream into our yard until there is hardly any place to park. My heart nearly stops when I see George and Anne drive in. Anne walks over by me and after a short hesitation, reaches out and hugs me. Then we, along with several other farmers' wives, begin to set up tables and chairs. We make sandwiches and lemonade as fast as we can to refresh the men. When one group leaves the barn for a break, another enters and so it goes for hours.

Fast work has the fire contained but not extinguished. The green hay that caused the fire keeps smoldering.

When Leslie and the girls get home from school, their bus struggles to get around all the vehicles in the yard. Most of the immediate danger has passed but the situation is still dangerous and we have to watch this well into the night – probably all night.

The next day the difficult task of digging out the burnt hay begins. As the blackened hay is freed from the haymow, its sickening odor nearly chokes us. The fire tries to rekindle and more water is poured on. Many wagon loads of the ruined hay are hauled out and spread on the fields.

Several days later, when all calms down, we realize just how close we came to losing our barn. How I thank God for early detection by Harvey and willing neighbors and friends to help us save it.

Family Picture 1951

CHAPTER FORTY EIGHT

"Leslie"

June 25, 1955, our Leslie and his Elaine are married. Hardly seems possible our son is twenty-two years old already, married and well into farming for his life's work. He and Dan get along about as good as any two generations. Some of their arguments remind me of how Dan and his dad went at each other. The old versus the new – who will win? As all good fathers and sons, one or the other gives way and I've noticed they take turns as to who does the giving in. That's as it should be.

We remodel the upstairs into a small apartment for the young couple. We add plumbing to the north bedroom to make it into a kitchen. The girls move downstairs to the small spare bedroom. It'll be hard on them because they're each used to having their own room. But Shirley is off to college this fall so Carol will have it most of the time.

"I don't think it's a good idea for two women to run one house. Never works. I remember when Olsons tried that. It was one argument after the other over who had the last word. Never works," Dan says.

"But we've all agreed on it except you," I reply. "Elaine has the say over their apartment upstairs and I have it down here. I don't understand your concern."

"Well, when the trouble starts, remember I was against it."

Then the dreaded letter from the Draft Board comes for Leslie. I sit and stare at it for a long time before I lay it on the table for him. Just married. Needed on the farm. I pray, "Oh, dear God, please let his rating be 4-F like it was the last time so he isn't drafted. Please."

When Leslie opens it, my prayer's answer is, "No." He is given 1-A and must report to Fort Leonard Wood, Missouri, in one month. My heart sinks and I do too – into the first chair I can find.

How things do go. Harvey wanted to go but when he had his physical, his eyesight wasn't good enough. He was rated 4-F. It just doesn't seem fair Leslie has to go when he is now married and settling into his life here on the farm.

Leslie leaves for boot camp and solemnly requests we take good care of Elaine for him. "But, of course we will," I say. "You didn't even have to ask."

Leslie's two-year service includes time in Missouri, Georgia and overseas in West Germany. Elaine takes a six-week leave of absence from work and spends it with Leslie in Germany.

Although it is a difficult separation, the time does pass and we all try our best to help Elaine handle it. The two years also give Leslie and Elaine time to plan and save for the future when they will take over the family farm.

CHAPTER FORTY NINE

"Harvey"

Harvey being the oldest son, we naturally hope he'll marry one day and settle down. He isn't interested in a life-long career in farming. He has many different girlfriends, but never gets serious about any of them. Sooner or later the girls sense their relationship with him is going nowhere and they move on to someone else. He, also, has his share of times when he ends the relationship.

Harvey is interested in the world of invention. An avid reader, he's studied all the greats – Edison, Franklin, the Wright Brothers, etc. And he has a real talent for getting his machines to work. Besides his Dad, he'll often have one of his friends help him. Hours and hours are spent in the workshop, nights and Sunday afternoons, developing one thing or another.

Although Harvey helps with the farm work, his heart is not in farming. He's not interested in college, although he attended a four-month farm short course out of high school. Perhaps it was there he discovered he didn't want to spend his life farming.

Hard as he works at his inventions, he never gets very far with any of them. Before long the friends helping him grow discouraged and stop coming over. He drops one idea to start another and spends a lot of time trying to solve the many, many obstacles in the way of any new development.

His bottom silo unloader invention is one that comes close to success. A company invests money for a test model and when the check comes in, we're so excited. Because development doesn't move along to the company's expectations, interest fades and the project is dropped.

We keep hoping he will soon find his niche in life and pursue it. Meanwhile, he helps out with the farm work.

CHAPTER FIFTY

"The Girls Move West"

The Sunday evening the girls asked to talk to me and Dan about plans to move to Colorado, I sure didn't like the idea. It would mean losing our girls. When would we ever see them? What are two little girls going to do when trouble comes and there are no parents to help them? These questions and more run through my mind.

"Why would you want to do such a thing?" I ask.

"Well, Mom, when we were out there on vacation in 1957, I met Cline," Carol says. "He's the biggest reason why I want to move out there. You met him last Christmas and seemed to approve of him. We're pretty serious about each other. Besides with him close by, he can help us if we ever need anything."

"People are different out there, Mom," says Shirley. "They're so much more friendly and we like the life of ranching and riding horses whenever we want. We want to send for Dixie Lea just as soon as we get settled. Then we'll just have to rent one horse to go riding. To tell you the truth, we felt more at home out there as far as life style goes than we ever did here in Wisconsin."

When the girls go up to bed, I slump down lower on the couch to think. Dan mumbles something about this being just a phase they're going through and they will get over it soon. He goes off to bed. But I think back two years ago to 1957. The girls spent a week at this dude ranch near Colorado Springs. Shirley had met a girl at college who raved about life in the west, and that's where they got the idea to vacation out there. The girls so being into their horses naturally fell in love with the idea of spending a whole week riding and living in the Colorado mountains. That first year I even had to call in for Shirley and ask her boss for an additional week's vacation so they could stay longer. And Carol met Cline.

The next year they went back for two weeks and Carol and Cline's relationship grew. They'd written to each other the entire year in between and he'd come for Christmas. Nice boy. We all like him. Now they want to move out there.

As I'm buried in these memories, Harvey comes in from his date. "Hi, Mom," he says. "How come you're up so late?"

"The girls just announced to me and Dad that they want to move to Colorado this spring."

"No. Don't tell me they've fallen for all the nonsense they've been told on that dude ranch? Don't they know those people do anything to make their stay great so they'll come back again? Real life would never be like that."

"I know. I know. Would you talk to them and see if you can get that through to them? I'm afraid they're disillusioned a bit and are believing life out there will be like their vacations were."

"I'll have a chat with them soon as I can. That's way too far for two girls only 20 and 22 to be going."

The next weekend, as I'm tidying up the living room, I hear Harvey talking to Shirley in the girls' bedroom.

"Why should I listen to anything you have to say?" Shirley snaps. "You've never cared a bit about me all these years. All you've done to me and Carol is criticize us. We never do a thing right in your or Leslie's eyes. So don't try coming around now as the big concerned brother."

Before Harvey can say another word, Shirley stomps out of the bedroom and goes out the front door.

That June the girls and I pack up their 1955 Oldsmobile 88 and drive out to Colorado Springs, Colorado. They'd written a letter to the

Colorado State Employment Office and were told jobs were available and they should get in contact when they arrive.

I stay at the dude ranch with them for a day and then return home by train. One of the hardest things I've ever had to do in my life was to leave my two daughters in such a strange place so far away from home. But they're old enough to be out on their own so I pray God will be with them. I know he will – I just need to keep praying for my own sake as well. Life is going to be so different without them around.

CHAPTER FIFTY ONE

"House on the Lake"

Leslie and Elaine sit across the table from me and Dan, a serious look on their faces. They want to buy all the personal property (machinery and livestock) on the farm. Eventually they hope to buy the land. Dan and I will move to a small two-bedroom cottage on Lake Poygan, just five miles from the farm. Leslie asks Dan, "I'd like you to come help when you can work it in. I know your tiling business will keep you pretty busy but there will be times when I'll need your help."

"Sure," Dan says nodding his head.

March 1st we pack our things and move to the lake. With the boys, Elaine and our friends, the Davies, we get it all done in one day. How I'm going to love taking care of a smaller house. I enjoy looking at the water out the living room bay window. It's never still and I find that so interesting.

Our Rusty is getting old now and prefers laying around nearly all the time. We talk to Leslie about leaving him at the farm he knows so well. A move to a small yard by a lake wouldn't be good for him when he's used to the space of a farm yard. Leslie agrees so Rusty stays behind. Dan will be at the farm nearly every day so Rusty won't feel abandoned. I'll miss him but I know he'll be happier there.

Dan retires from farming, but that spring begins work in his tiling business. When he'd learned of this tiling business being for sale with the seller's clients included, he put in a bid for the business. It was accepted. We hope it will bring in enough income to live reasonably well. He leaves early every morning and doesn't get home until after dark.

My days are filled with taking care of my small house and tending to my flower garden. I find life at the lake far different from the hustle and bustle of the farm. Although I miss some of that activity, I'm so much more relaxed here at the lake.

Then one day on a walk to the mailbox, things change. I'm halfway there, about half a city block, when a huge Great Dane and two Weimaraners come loping across the neighbor's yard. I stand still in shock, knowing I dare not try to outrun them. They gallop up to me, sniffing but wagging their stubby tails and I realize they aren't vicious, just curious. I put my hand out and talk softly. They circle me a couple times, their tongues hanging out and then lope off to the next neighbor's yard. When my heart settles down again, I continue to the mailbox and then return to the house wondering what kind of people we have next door that allow such animals to run loose.

As time goes on, I become friends with these beasts by giving them scraps of food. They aren't really a threat to me except for their size and unexpected visits. Dan and I are going to have to talk to these people.

CHAPTER FIFTY TWO

"Double Wedding"

Carol and Cline are engaged soon after the girls move out West. Shirley meets Rod, a friend of Cline's, and they are engaged the next March. Because of their close friendship, they want a double wedding. Another reason the girls like this idea is because Dan and I were married that way. Preparation for the wedding is easy because they only want a church wedding followed by a dinner in the church basement.

The girls settle on a ranch near Colorado Springs where both boys work. Rod drives a semi-trailer truck and hauls horses and cattle all over the state and beyond. Cline is a ranch hand caring for the animals at the ranch. The girls continue in their jobs, Carol as a secretary in the X-ray Department of Colorado Community Hospital and Shirley in Civil Service at Ent Air Force Base.

All goes well until the middle of August. I'm just recovering from the flu – finally able to get out of bed and do some of my housework, when I get a call from Shirley.

"Rod's gone," she says and begins to sob.

"Gone," I exclaim. "What do you mean?"

"He wa—wa—was to be home two weeks ago and ne—ne—never came. I got a call from hi—hi—his boss asking me if there was any trouble in our marriage. I said 'no' and then he told me a rancher found the semi parked by the side of the road and no Rod."

Shirley breaks down sobbing a few minutes and my heart nearly stops.

"I- I di- didn't call so- sooner bc- because I hoped he'd come back. I- I guess he must be OK because Mr. Bryce has a signed gas slip in his credit card statement dated three days after Rod went missing. Oh, Mom, what am I going to do?"

I'm shaking so hard I have to find a chair so I say, "Hold on a minute. I'll be right back."

I slowly pull the desk chair out and sit down. My mind races as to what to say.

"I'm back, Shirley."

Shirley continues, "Carol and I went to the police and told them about him being missing and they weren't one bit concerned. They said there was nothing they could do in a case like this. Just what does it mean – 'a case like this?' Oh, Mom, I feel so helpless."

I try to comfort my girl as best I can and shakily hang up the phone.

When Dan gets home I tell him the awful news and say, "What are we going to do?"

"Don't know as there's much we can do," Dan says.

"What about hiring a detective to find out what happened to him?" I ask.

"And how do we afford such a thing? Give him some time. I'm sure he'll be back," says Dan.

The end of September I take the train out to help Shirley. Both girls come to pick me up, their faces grim. Shirley is so thin and pale. On the way to the ranch the girls talk nonstop. As we come over the last hill to the small ranch house, I see Carol and Cline's mobile home parked near it. We go into the house and the girls explain they have called every possible contact Rod could have had the past month. Whenever someone had a lead, it wound up as a dead end. No one knew where he went.

The week I'm there, Shirley has problems being sick to her stomach a few times and I begin to suspect she might be pregnant. We talk about it and she promises to see a doctor soon.

A week later, I reluctantly leave my girls and return home. Shirley calls me a few days after I'm home to announce she is indeed pregnant and expects her baby the middle of May. Sad as things are for her right now, I'm so excited to hear I'm to become a grandma for the first time. Something good is coming out of this dismal state of affairs.

That Christmas Dan and I drive out to Colorado to spend it with the girls. We talk to Mr. Bryce and hear his idea on the situation. It's obvious Rod has just taken off and only time will tell if he'll ever return. Plans are made for Shirley to return to Wisconsin after the baby is born. She will find work and I will take care of the baby. Shirley tries hard to put on a good front – that she is alright – but I can see how devastated she really is.

Because Rod no longer works on the ranch, Shirley has to leave the ranch house by the first of the year. Dan and I help her find a small mobile home in a trailer court on the outskirts of Colorado Springs. It's just thirty feet long, but the $30/month rent is something she can afford.

The drive home is a long and sad one. My eyes fill with tears off and on as I fight with myself over the difficulty my daughter is in. How I pray God will be with her and help her through these next few months.

CHAPTER FIFTY THREE

"My First Grandchild"

All through the long months between Christmas and May, I write letters of encouragement to Shirley. She writes often and leads me to believe she is doing fine. She is taking knitting classes and spends her evenings learning the various stitches. She continues to play organ at her church every Sunday and to teach Sunday School. When I call her, she sounds as though she's coping fairly well, but I know from her letters that she's having a hard time accepting what has happened to her.

She's decided to call a daughter Carrie but needs help picking a second name and I suggest she call her Carrie Lynn. She likes that and thanks me for helping her decide. A son's name will be Timothy Daniel.

The middle of February, Shirley calls to tell us a rancher in Arizona had called Cline asking for references on Rod. She wants to go down and see him so she asks that we wire her some extra money. She calls the rancher the night before she is to leave and finds Rod has already left. Another dead end.

Difficult as all this is, at least we now know for sure that Rod is alive and apparently well.

The baby is due May 15 so the end of April, I again take the train to Colorado Springs to be with Shirley. Although two people living in a 30-ft. trailer is rather cramped, we spend a lot of time away seeing sights and shopping. And we play Canasta.

May 25, 1961, Carrie Lynn is born. She enters the world causing her mother much difficulty but with expert medical care, Shirley and her baby are fine. And I'm the proudest Grandma in the world!

We return to Wisconsin the July 4th weekend.

CHAPTER FIFTY FOUR

"Precious Moments"

It's moments like this I so enjoy with my little granddaughter. She loves to be rocked to sleep for her naps and I love rocking her. As I hold her, I'm taken back to when my own children were babies – such wonderful times. What a joy it is to relive those precious moments.

I'm holding her in my left arm, her bottle with my right hand. Her eyes are closed as she's nearly asleep yet her little fingers still hold tightly to my finger on the hand holding the bottle. She has soft brown, curly hair and is so content. Soon I slowly take the bottle away and set it on the end table. Although she's asleep, I can't lay her down yet. I'm going to hold her for just a little while longer. Before I know it, she won't want to be held like this, so I'm going to treasure every moment.

Carol is expecting her first baby in October. I convince Shirley to stay home with Carrie until after Carol has her baby. Once she starts a job, she won't have time to enjoy her little one like she is now. And she will miss so much being gone every day. We'll go out and help Carol with her baby and after that, Shirley can start work.

My thoughts drift back to how I felt when the girls married. They were going to live so far away. I grieved over the fact I would hardly ever see their children. Leslie and Elaine don't seem interested in starting a family. Whenever I mention it to them, I get this silent treatment. My grandchildren will never get to know me seeing me only a few days or weeks a year.

I listen to our friends brag about their grandchildren and now have one of my own to brag about. Never did I dream though, that I'd have a grandchild right in my own home. What a joy! I thank God for this precious little one who has not only brought such happiness to Shirley, but to me and Dan. She's so alone with Rod gone and Carol and Cline so far away but having her little daughter means she will never be alone again.

Carol's baby girl, Catherine Julie, is born October 9. The visit to Colorado brings joy in seeing another grandchild - so tiny with dark hair and eyes. I try to help Carol with the way I cared for my babies. I tell her, "When you give her a bath, put your left arm under her head at the elbow and hold her left arm with your hand. That way she can't slip away from you."

"Really," says Carol. "Shirley, is that the way you give Carrie a bath?"

"Yes. That works really well," says Shirley.

"Breast milk is the best thing for a baby," I say.

"How long did you breast feed Carrie, Shirley?" Carol asks.

I notice that no matter what I say to help Carol, she checks with Shirley about everything and finally I just let the two of them talk about things. This makes me feel like I might as well have stayed home. We leave with me trying very hard not to feel sad.

We return home the end of October. November 2 Shirley begins her job as a secretary with Medical Associates – a small five-doctor medical clinic in Menasha. She will be driving twelve miles one way to work each day.

CHAPTER FIFTY FIVE

"Shirley's New Home"

On the way home from church one fine spring Sunday, I'm deep in thought about pastor's sermon on forgiveness. Then I remember the dog trouble and say to Dan, "We have to do something soon about those neighbor dogs. I can't relax a minute when I take Carrie outside. When can we get the fence up?"

"I've been thinking about that," Dan says. "How about a white picket fence? I've always thought they look nice."

"Oh that'd be just fine."

"I'll get the wood next Saturday when I'm at the co-op."

I don't like Dan putting up a fence at all but we tried to talk to these people about keeping their animals in their own yard and it did no good. All the neighbors are upset not only with the dogs themselves, but the messes they leave behind. Several of the neighbors have contacted the village authorities who in turn warned the Sawyers but the problem goes on.

Dan puts up a beautiful white picket fence. It runs the entire one hundred fifty feet from the lake to the road on the west side of our property. It will give us time to get to the house while the dogs run around to the end of the fence on their way into our yard.

Shirley and I often take a walk after supper. One night she says, "Mom, you remember how I want to get a place of my own some day?"

"Yes, I remember," I answer.

"Well, I may have a chance to get a used mobile home soon. Do you think it'd be possible to put it on the north side of your lot? Would you and Dad mind?"

"No. We wouldn't mind. I think it might work. How big is it?"

"Ten by fifty."

"Our lot runs 150 feet so I certainly don't see any problem. Let's talk to Dad about it."

The doctor selling the mobile home lived in it while waiting to divorce his wife. He wants $2,000. Shirley has $1,000 saved and needs to borrow the rest from the bank. She is able to only with the doctor co-signing the note.

The mobile home is delivered the end of April and Shirley and two-year-old Carrie move in. How empty the house is without them at night or on the weekends. Close as they still are, I miss having them right in the house.

Carrie is such a darling at this age. She talks a mile a minute, loves her stuffed animals and is such a joy to take care of.

When I get my hair done each week at Izma's Beauty Parlor, I take her along. She's so good, plays in the corner of the room with her animals and books. Oh, how she loves looking through her books and she loves it when we read to her.

"Let's go down to Milwaukee Saturday," I say to Shirley when she comes home to pick Carrie up that night.

"Oh, yeah – let's. That'd be fun. I love our shopping trips. Carrie and I both need some things. This Saturday would be great because Friday is payday. That means I'll have some money," Shirley says with a grin.

Shirley does the driving and we have a ball talking about anything and everything but our troubles. We've made it a rule to leave our troubles at home – forget them for a day. Carrie naps most of the one-and-one-half hour trip down and when we shop, is content to sit in her stroller watching the people while hugging her teddy bear.

We have lunch at one of the mall restaurants and about mid-afternoon head home. We're refreshed again and ready to take on whatever lies ahead.

August 1, 1963, Carol and Cline's second daughter, Cindy Jean, is born. This time Shirley and Carrie stay home and I go out to help Carol alone. Cindy is a darling baby with lots of curly black hair. She is a frail little thing and has a mild birth defect that consists of a swelling around her left elbow. The doctors say it isn't anything serious and advises nothing be done. She will have no problem using her arm.

Shirley and me

CHAPTER FIFTY SIX

"Divorced"

The end of January, 1964, Shirley and I go to court for her divorce. She had to live in Wisconsin two years before she could get one and although it bothered her at first, the two years did go by fast. The judge wonders if Rod may have died and Shirley should receive life insurance but when he's told of the times we'd heard he was alive, he lets it go and grants her the divorce.

Shirley still seems devastated over Rod's leaving. I'm afraid her broken heart isn't going to heal very fast. She never talks about dating or going out to meet anybody. I pray that one day someone worthy of her will come along.

Meanwhile she is totally absorbed in her career and her daughter. She's determined to reach the top at the clinic which is adding two new doctors this fall. She took a correspondence course in Medical Shorthand last year which she says has helped her and she often takes evening classes in Human Relations and Supervision.

The next spring Pastor asks Shirley to play organ again. She played three years before moving West and now the organist who replaced her then is leaving. Four-year-old Carrie will sit on a little chair right next to the organ bench while Shirley plays.

CHAPTER FIFTY SEVEN

"Dog Trouble"

This fall Carrie starts kindergarten and loves school. One Saturday night Shirley calls very upset, "Mom, one of those Sawyer dogs bit Carrie on the shoulder today. I saw the dogs were out and called her in and as she ran to the house, one came up and bit her. I found teeth marks on her shoulder when she took her bath tonight. What if she'd turned her head? He'd have bitten her in the face. We have to do something before she really gets hurt."

The next night Dan calls the Sawyers and asks them to come over to Shirley's mobile home and talk about what happened. I walk the floor wondering how things are going over there and when Dan gets back home, he tells me only Bob Sawyer came over. But they explained the situation to him and asked him to please restrain their animals. He nodded and acted like he would.

However, the next night, Jan Sawyer visits Shirley. When she leaves, Shirley comes over and says, "She came in the house asking, 'What's this about my dogs?' Apparently Bob hadn't told her a thing about the discussion the night before."

Shirley went on, "I explained how one of her dogs bit Carrie on the shoulder and this woman sat on the couch, tears running down her cheeks saying how everyone is down on her wonderful animals. She said, 'Do you know since we've lived here all we've had is trouble with the people living around here? They're so mean to my dogs. Don't they realize how many skunks and river rats they've kept away from their yards? Why, we've even had people poke sticks at them through the fence on the west side of our house. Why can't people realize that they aren't going to hurt anybody? Carrie should never have run away from my dog. Because she did she caused him to nip at her. How come you haven't taught her to stand still when a dog comes running up to her? He'll only sniff her over a little, that's all.' Can you believe that, Mom?"

The next school day, Carrie comes home from the bus crying. She wants to go into the mobile home and get all her stuffed animals. As she's gathering them in her arms and handing some to me to carry, she mumbles, "I can't let them burn up Grandma. Lisa told me they're going to burn down our trailer."

Lisa is the youngest of the Sawyer's three children and often came over to play with Carrie. But on the bus tonight, Lisa told Carrie her mom and dad plan to burn down the trailer because we're against their dogs.

That night I tell Dan what happened and say, "We have to do something about these dogs. Can't you call somebody?"

"Well, people have tried that and it gets them nowhere. All it does is build up resentment. We tried it and look how they've taken it? They just get angry and defend their animals. Nobody is going to do anything so stupid as start any fire. Let's wait a while and see if it doesn't blow over."

The next week we receive a letter in the mail. It's from an attorney informing us that our picket fence has to be moved two feet to the east. The neighbors had their lot lines checked and found we put the fence on their property. Dan tries to reason with them over such a small fraction, but they insist he move the fence. So he does.

Dan is right about things blowing over. They finally do and Lisa comes over to play again. Seeing Dan struggle moving the fence must have been revenge enough for these people. It isn't until they move away though that the dog problem is solved.

CHAPTER FIFTY EIGHT

"Changes on the Farm"

One night while Dan and I are eating supper, Shirley comes in the door and slams it behind her.

"Do you know Leslie bought the Thompson farm?" she blurts.

"What?" Dan says as he jerks his head up from his plate.

"I just stopped in there and Leslie told me he bought the Thompson farm yesterday. When I asked him if you knew about it, he said 'yes.' What happened? I thought they were buying the family farm?"

I sat there for a few moments in shock and then say, "Well, I guess it really doesn't surprise me. We weren't getting too far with our negotiations. Seemed like they were in a big hurry to have them signed and I wanted to think things over more."

Turns out Leslie and Elaine grew weary of waiting for us and thought we weren't really interested in selling to them. This, of course, is not true but now that he's bought the farm adjacent to ours, there isn't a thing we can do about it.

This means we're left with 200 acres of land and the buildings, but no personal property. Who's going to want an empty farm? These days when people buy a place they want it furnished.

When Harvey finds out what Leslie and Elaine have done, he says, "I'll rent some of the land from you. Have some machinery of my own and I'll get whatever else I need."

One day Dan comes home to tell me Rusty is gone. Dan says, "I was working in the machine shop on that axle when I heard a tractor go by and Rusty yelp. I ran out to see that kid Leslie has working for him sitting on the tractor, looking down at something in back of him.

I went to see and it was Rusty. He'd run him over with that tractor. I fired him on the spot. He knew that dog was old and couldn't be getting out of the way very fast but he didn't think and drove that tractor way too fast in the yard. When I knelt down by Rusty he was already dead."

I put my arms around Dan and we both stand there grieving the loss of the best dog we ever had. The thought that maybe we shouldn't have left him behind ran through my mind but there's no sense in thinking like that now. It's too late. Poor Rusty!

Harvey now lives with us at the lake as his apartment was costing him too much.

He's finished with his contract at Thilmany Pulp and Paper so will have time on his hands and is able to do some farming. He'll also help Dan with his tiling business when needed.

Renting some of the property to Harvey is a help but he often has a hard time making the payments and owning the land is now a problem for us. We won't have the income Leslie was paying for using all of it and we will need to rent out the house to get some income.

Carol and Cline's third daughter, Corine Hildegarde, arrives November 26, 1968. They now live in Arkansas where they purchased some land. Being close to Cline's family in Louisiana, I assume his family will help her with the new baby and don't go to help. Turns out she had no extra help with this little one. When I hear this, I feel sad that I didn't go like I did for Cathy and Cindy.

After thirteen years of marriage, Leslie and Elaine's son, Robert Daniel, is born on May 13, 1969. Elaine had been working as an Executive Secretary at Kimberly-Clark Corporation but elects to stay home and raise her son. Now I'll have two grandchildren close to me – my Carrie and now Robert.

In December, 1969, Shirley starts dating again. She meets Terry Schroeder who worked with Harvey at Thilmany Pulp and Paper Company. She invites him to meet us on their fourth date and I think he's quite a gentleman. I'm happy for Shirley.

In the spring of 1972, Carol and Cline decide to move to Wisconsin. They talk to me and Dan about living on the farm and renting the land. We have had no end of grief from the renters we've put in that house so it will be nice to have responsible people living there. Harvey is willing that Cline rent the land as farming didn't work out very well for him.

When Carol and her family move home, I can hardly believe I have all my children and grandchildren around me. At the time the girls moved away, I thought I'd never see the day this would happen. I'm so happy it has.

August 2, 1972, Leslie and Elaine's second son, Peter William, is born. Now we have six wonderful grandchildren.

Granddaughters:
Corine
(in my arms),
Carrie,
Cathy
and Cindy

Cathy, Carrie and me

Me and 6-year-old Carrie

CHAPTER FIFTY NINE

"Dan's Illness"

Lately I notice Dan seems to be hard of hearing. I talk to him and he often doesn't answer me. I ask him things and he looks away. If he can't hear, it would make sense with his being around that loud tiling machine every day. In the night I often hear him rummaging through the medicine cabinet in the bathroom. When I ask what's wrong, he mumbles something about a headache.

One afternoon Carol stops over to talk to me about Dan. She says, "Daddy's been acting strange when he stops at the farm. Sometimes he walks by me without a word. Then he'll sit a while on the couch and hold his head in his hands. The other day I helped him in the shop and he asked for a screw driver when he meant a hammer. Does he act like this at home, Mom?"

I say, "Not exactly but it seems like he can't hear. Do you think that's it?"

"Gee. I'll have to keep that in mind. But, Mom, I think he needs to see a doctor. Deer hunting is coming up and what's he going to do off in the woods all alone?"

Dan goes deer hunting and I worry more than ever about him. He does come home safe and sound but the hearing and headaches seem to be worse.

The next Friday Carol calls, "Mom, we have to get Dad to the doctor. He's laying on the couch holding his head and moaning. I've called Shirley to get him in at the clinic this afternoon. I'm taking him in as soon as she calls to give me the time."

I hang up the phone and stagger to the couch shaking and sobbing, "Oh dear God, please help my Dan."

Dan is diagnosed with a brain tumor. He is admitted to the hospital December 20 with surgery scheduled for the day after Christmas.

Christmas Day we all meet in Dan's hospital room to have dinner with him. When Shirley and Terry arrive, Shirley hugs me and then puts her left hand in my face. She's wearing a diamond ring. They'd gotten engaged just before coming for dinner. When Shirley first shows her ring to Dan, he just looks away. The next time she tries, he grabs her hand and smiles from ear to ear. Then he looks at Terry and raises his hand to shake Terry's. He mutters something we can't understand, but we can tell by his action that he knows what it means. One happy moment during this sad business.

December 26 Dan has surgery but the surgeon cannot remove the entire tumor. He takes out what he can and says it will grow back. We take Dan home for the two months they predict he will live.

One night Shirley comes over in tears to tell me Dan had asked her when she and Terry were going to get married. When she told him August, he wondered why so far off. She explained that Carrie still needs to be with me for the summer. I try to comfort her as we both realize Dan will be gone by her wedding day.

Dan gets along quite well the next four months – well past the two they gave him. But I worry about him every minute of the day. I watch when he walks around the yard to be sure he doesn't stumble and fall. I try hard to be near him when he gets up from the chair or couch just in case he stumbles. I won't let him drive to the farm but drive him there and back myself.

Early April, Easter time, Dan begins to show more signs of deterioration. When he talks, I can't understand what he says. He can't write. On my birthday, April 16, I can't read the scribbles on the birthday card Shirley bought for him to give me.

By the beginning of May he is down in bed and only up to the bathroom. Soon I can't handle him alone for that and need Harvey or Shirley to help get him to and from the bathroom. By the next week he is bedridden. He won't eat. He only sips water now and then. When I give him a bath he favors his right arm so much that if I even touch it, he winces and moans. So I try not to touch that arm. He can't talk – only stares at the wall and I sit holding his hand, crying. Now and then he pats me on the head as if he understands my sorrow but there is no way he can.

The afternoon of May 16, Dan falls into a coma. That evening, with all our children present, he stops breathing.

CHAPTER SIXTY

"What I Have Left"

The weeks after Dan's funeral are nothing but a blur. I vaguely remember Carrie and Cathy's Confirmation Day – even though the dinner is held here at my home. I put in an appearance but my mind is elsewhere.

A visit with the attorney temporarily settles my finances and Harvey is named Executor of the Estate. I must trust he'll do fine with the help of the attorney. Dan didn't have a will and I guess this causes problems but I don't really understand what they are nor do I care. I'm just existing one day at a time.

Harvey is here most of the time which is a comfort. For the first time in my sixty-five years, I'm afraid to be alone. All those years on the farm – a mile from any civilization, a woods behind the buildings, salesmen driving into the yard at any time – never bothered me. Of course, I also had Rusty to protect me. But now that I'm older, I'm afraid a lot of the time – especially nights.

By August I have found life without Dan to be bearable only because I try hard to think of my children and grandchildren. By August 16, Shirley and Terry's Wedding Day, I'm feeling more like myself.

The end of August Carrie and Shirley move to their new home in Neenah. I keep telling myself it is only ten miles away – easy to see them – or for them to see me. But, of course, it's not the same. Happy as I am for Shirley, I worry about Carrie. With them marrying, she's the one who has to make the most adjustment. Sure, Terry always treated her well the years they dated but is he ready for a fourteen-year-old daughter? So I call her often. I have her come stay over the weekend now and then. She tells me she's fine but I still wonder.

Harvey is involved in sales work now. He calls it "pyramid" something or other. He listens to motivational tapes so loud sometimes that I could scream. When he takes trips and is away nights, I get one of Carol's girls to stay with me so I'm not alone.

I meet with my attorney to draw up a will. I feel because Dan didn't have one, problems occurred which could have been avoided. But I'm more concerned about Harvey. My other three children are settled in life and taking care of themselves and their families. He's so alone and dependent on me. He's a big help to me and yet any employment he tries never seems to take care of him.

In my will I want the house at the lake to go to all four children but with the understanding that Harvey can live there as long as he wants. That should take care of him.

I often give Harvey money because he's such a help to me. When I write the checks I call it "wages" because to me, he's earned every cent.

CHAPTER SIXTY ONE

"Another Grandson"

July 26, 1976, Shirley and Terry's son, Daniel Ralph, is born. What a day this was. Shirley had a difficult time having him – was in the hospital from 4:00 a.m. until 7:00 p.m. before he was born. Carrie called me midmorning and was upset because she hadn't heard anything from the hospital so I went down to be with her. We went to the hospital and they let us talk to Shirley for a few minutes which helped Carrie feel better. Me too.

Shirley has decided to quit her job as Assistant Administrator of the clinic, the position she worked hard to achieve the last fifteen years, and stay home to raise Daniel.

May 4, 1977, Carol and Cline's son, Clint Daniel, is born. Now I have four granddaughters and four grandsons. How Dan would have enjoyed these wonderful grandchildren.

One evening Carol and Cline come over and announce they would like to buy the farm. During the settling of the estate, a price had been put on it low enough for them to purchase it. They've applied for a loan through the FHA people. I say, "Well, if you can meet the price the estate has, I guess it's fine. Let me talk to everybody and see what they all think."

I talk to Harvey and he has no interest in nor does he have the finances to buy the place. Leslie feels the farm is worth more than what it was appraised for when the estate was settled. Shirley has no interest in it with her Terry being an electrical engineer.

Papers are drawn up and I sign them, happy the farm will stay in the family.

I visit Dan's grave whenever I'm shopping in Oshkosh. As I put flowers in the vase, I mutter, "Oh, Dan, you shouldn't be here yet."

How well I remember the day he and I drove around and decided this was the cemetery where we wanted to buy lots. It's unique in that the grave stones are flush with the ground so all you see are vases full of flowers. Dan had said, "Looks more like a garden than a cemetery. I like that."

And so here he is now – age 69 – far too young. Tears come and I know it's time to leave.

CHAPTER SIXTY TWO

"First Signs"

Shopping trips with Shirley and little Danny are such fun. Reminds me of when Carrie was his age and we'd go on our trips. Now she's in high school and far too busy to be doing much shopping with Mom and Grandma.

Danny is so good in the restaurants – as Carrie always was. Both children were taken to restaurants from little on so they learned how to behave. Today, I don't feel very well though. My stomach needs coffee I guess. Yet again, I feel so full – like I've overeaten when I haven't. I've been seeing one of the doctors at the clinic where Shirley worked. I'll have to ask him what this could mean.

At my next visit to Dr. Haskins, I mention my distress. He tells me it's probably gas buildup. He advises me to watch what I eat and see if I can pin down any certain food that might be bothering me this way.

Spring, 1979, Carrie and Cathy graduate from high school. How fast those four years went. Carrie's graduation party is right after the ceremony and I make it to her party. But I can't attend Cathy's, set for the next day, because I enter Theda Clark Hospital for tests.

CHAPTER SIXTY THREE

"Last Days"

I endure one test after another with none of them revealing a thing. Yet I still have this bloated feeling. All I can do is trust I'm OK and carry on. After five days I go home.

I drag myself through each day with the sensation still there and have little appetite. I find myself laying down a lot and feeling there has to be something wrong somewhere.

Mid-August Shirley goes along with me to see Dr. Haskins. He asks, "How're you doing?" I say, "Pretty well. I'm able to do my dishes now, - -" Shirley butts in with "She's not doing well at all, Dr. Haskins. She's tired and weak and has no appetite. And she's losing weight. Something is wrong."

Dr. Haskins says to me, "Excuse me a minute."

He and Shirley leave but I can hear them out in the hall.

Dr. Haskins says, "Looks like she's regressing and the reason may not be good. I need her back in the hospital." I don't hear Shirley's reply but when they come back in the room, he says "I need to have you back in the hospital for more tests. Can I send you right over to Theda Clark?"

I nod and Shirley says, "I'll go get your things, Mom, and bring them to you."

This time I was subjected to a horrible test where they put a long tube down my throat. Even though they froze my throat, I was awake and felt it going down. I thought I would choke.

Dr. Haskins comes to me that afternoon while Shirley is with me and tells me I have a small tumor in my stomach. I will need surgery to remove it and they schedule it two days from now.

Somehow I can't handle this news. Last thing I want to go through is surgery and I remember Dan and what happened to him. Will the results be the same for me? Sleep doesn't come at night and I lay there tossing and turning until they strap me in the bed. This restraint takes me back to horror stories about when Hitler took over Germany and I'm back there hiding from him. I try with all my might to get out of the straps but I can't. The more I struggle, the more afraid I become.

What's going to happen to me? I must get out of here. I must. When a nurse visits me, I beg for a knife so I can cut the straps and free myself. I have to before the Nazis get me.

The morning of my surgery, I feel calm. The straps are taken off, I'm transferred to another cart and wheeled away. Shirley and Carol walk beside my cart to the surgical ward.

I awaken in ICU. First thing I see is a nurse bending over me calling my name over and over. I try to answer but feel so groggy, sluggish. Finally I can speak and say, "Hello. I'm OK. I'm OK." The nurse smiles and pats me on the shoulder. She says, "Good girl."

Later that afternoon, back in my room with Shirley by my side, Dr. Haskins walks in. He looks very serious and says, "The surgeon found a tumor in your stomach but that was only a small portion of a large tumor behind your stomach. They removed what they could but they couldn't take it all. It will grow back."

"Well," I say to Dr. Haskins, "Don't look so sad. Looks like I'm going to be in for a new adventure." I turn away thinking, "So I'm going to have the same future they gave my Dan."

The girls take me home and ask if there's anything I'd like to do with the time I have left. I say, "I'd like to go up north once more."

"When?"

"Oh, I don't know. I'll tell you when."

Shirley comes to stay with me every morning and Carol comes every afternoon. Harvey is here nights so I'm never alone.

I grow weaker and weaker every day and soon realize I'll never get up north.

CHAPTER SIXTY FOUR

"To Sleep"

People come to see me. Pastor brings tapes of his sermons. I enjoy hearing them and pretend I'm in church. How I miss going to God's house. Gretchen comes several times and Loren, Dan's brother-in-law who married his sister Mabel. Loren brings me copies of his son, Gerald's sermons but I don't really care to read anything. I prefer the tapes my Pastor brings.

There are times when both my girls are here and we have coffee together.

One day Elaine comes and tearfully tells me how sorry she and Leslie are that they didn't buy the family farm. I tell her, "It's OK. It was probably for the best. Carol and Cline have a reason to be in Wisconsin because of it and that's good."

Soon though, I don't want anyone around me but my children. I'm sure to be put in a nursing home any day – easier on everyone if I am.

I sleep a lot – don't want anything to eat or drink – not even my beloved coffee. I don't really hurt anywhere – the nurses in this home are so, so nice. Remind me of my girls who took such good care of me when I was still at home.

Where are my Harvey, Leslie, Shirley, Carol?

I feel so weary. Think I'll sleep a while.

AUTHOR'S EPILOG

Sunday, September 23, 1979, at 12:15 p.m., my wonderful mom died – at her home. She was laid to rest next to Daniel under their grave stone which appropriately states "Together Forever."

A FINAL WORD FROM THE AUTHOR

Fifteen years ago I enrolled in a creative writing class because I wanted to write this book about my mother's life. Along the way I attended writing seminars and joined writing groups so this dream could come true.

Over these fifteen years I was published forty times. Most of these stories were from my own life as a church organist, teacher's aide, avid sailboat racer, wife and mother.

The three years it took to write this book, I received help from my patient husband, my children, my brothers and sister and many writing friends. My thanks to them all!

AUTHOR'S EPILOG

Sunday, September 23, 1979, at 12:15 p.m., my wonderful mom died – at her home. She was laid to rest next to Daniel under their grave stone which appropriately states "Together Forever."

A FINAL WORD FROM THE AUTHOR

Fifteen years ago I enrolled in a creative writing class because I wanted to write this book about my mother's life. Along the way I attended writing seminars and joined writing groups so this dream could come true.

Over these fifteen years I was published forty times. Most of these stories were from my own life as a church organist, teacher's aide, avid sailboat racer, wife and mother.

The three years it took to write this book, I received help from my patient husband, my children, my brothers and sister and many writing friends. My thanks to them all!